Rowena Cherish

Victorian Servants
A Very Peculiar History™

With added elbow grease

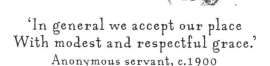

'In general we accept our place
With modest and respectful grace.'
Anonymous servant, c.1900

To all servants today

FMacD

Editor: Stephen Haynes
Editorial assistants: Rob Walker, Mark Williams
Additional artwork: Mark Bergin, Carolyn Franklin,
Penko Gelev, Nick Hewetson, John James, Gerald Wood

Published in Great Britain in MMXI by
Book House, an imprint of
The Salariya Book Company Ltd
25 Marlborough Place, Brighton BN1 1UB
www.salariya.com
www.book-house.co.uk

HB ISBN-13: 978-1-907184-49-9

© The Salariya Book Company Ltd MMXI

1 3 5 7 9 8 6 4 2
A CIP catalogue record for this book is available
from the British Library.
Printed and bound in Dubai.
Printed on paper from sustainable sources.

Visit our website at **www.book-house.co.uk**
or go to **www.salariya.com**
for **free** electronic versions of:
You Wouldn't Want to be an Egyptian Mummy!
You Wouldn't Want to be a Roman Gladiator!
You Wouldn't Want to be a Polar Explorer!
You Wouldn't Want to sail on a 19th-Century Whaling Ship!

Victorian Servants
A Very Peculiar History™

With added elbow grease

Ting!

Written by
Fiona Macdonald

Created and designed by
David Salariya

Illustrated by
David Antram

'No man is a hero to his servants.'

French writer and thinker
Michel de Montaigne (1533–1593)

'Good masters and mistresses [are]
quite as rare as good servants.'

British actress Fanny Kemble (1809–1893)

'A good mistress will make a
good servant.'

Popular Victorian saying

'Ladies and gentleman are permitted to
have friends in the kennel,[1] but not in
the kitchen.'[2]

Irish dramatist George Bernard Shaw
(1856–1950)

'The lowest work I think is honourable
in itself and the poor drudge[3] is
honourable too.'

Maid-of-all-work Hannah Cullwick
(1833–1909)

1. *among pet dogs and horses.*   2. *among servants.*
3. *hard-working servant.*

Contents

'The rich man in his castle,
The poor man at his gate,
God made them, high or lowly,
And ordered their estate.'

From the hymn 'All Things Bright and Beautiful', written by Mrs C. F. Alexander in 1848.*

All Victorians knew their place

* In the very same year, the Communist Manifesto by Karl Marx and Friedrich Engels was published in London. It called for a revolution to make everyone equal and give power to working people.

INTRODUCTION

'The greatest plague in life'[1]

Imagine! You've travelled back in time to 1860, and you're a woman servant. You've been working extra-hard this month, cleaning 83 pairs of dirty boots, plus all the windows and mirrors, in addition to your usual household duties. Looking down, you remark, with pride in all you have done, that 'My hands are very coarse and hardish.' But then your employer comes along. Her hands are white and soft. Although it's July, 'She lays her hand[s] lightly on mine for me to feel how cold they are.'[2]

1. Title of a humorous book about badly behaved servants by Augustus and Henry Mayhew, 1847.
2. from the diary of Hannah Cullwick (see pages 51 and 88).

What's going on? Is your employer unwell? Is she lonely or asking for sympathy? Has she had bad news, or a sudden shock? Or is her fine dress just too thin for a chilly English summer?

No, no, no, no and no. We're puzzled, but you, the servant, understand the gesture. Your employer's gentle, delicate touch is really a stern warning. She's keeping you in your place; reminding you who you are. 'We [servants] say it's to show the difference, more than anything.'

What difference? Not just the contrast between hands: white and rough, smooth and hard, workaday and leisured. But also the vast, unbridgeable social gap between 'them' and 'us'; between Victorian employers and their servants.

The Victorian age (1837–1901) was a time when more British people than ever before worked as domestic (household) servants. It was also a time when more British families than in any earlier era had servants to look after them. In this book we will look at the

men and women who joined in this Victorian servant 'population explosion'. What were their lives like?

Who were the 'servant classes' (as the Victorians called them)? Where did they come from? How did they find a job? And why on earth did they leave the freedom of their own homes and families to live in someone else's household? Even more perplexing: how could clever, capable, thinking, feeling, fully grown men and women let themselves be ordered around – and despised, as in the true story above – by people who were richer, grander, more powerful than themselves?

Today, looking back, we find the Victorian choice to spend a life obediently 'in service' very hard to understand. But we must remember: almost all servants could be sure, while they worked, of life's three great essentials – food, clothes and lodgings. Some also found companionship and care from colleagues and/or employers – though many other Victorian men and women were not so lucky, as we shall see.

Without whom...

To Victorian employers, servants were rather like troublesome teenage children: an expense, a worry, a responsibility, to be kept out of sight for as much of the time as possible. But they were essential.

The Victorian age was a time of great advances in science, medicine, industry, technology, travel, exploration, media, art and design. Unlike their employers, servants did not make exciting discoveries, run great companies, pass important new laws or conquer a mighty empire – but they cared for (and cleaned up after) every single one of the people who did. Without servants, the Victorian age would have been very different.

So let's hear it, then, for them all!

To servants! Without whom...

Worn out and thrown away

Sad to say – and shockingly, to modern eyes – a long lifetime of loyal service was not always rewarded. Though some servants were looked after by their employers until death, in Victorian law this was not compulsory. Many masters and mistresses dismissed servants who were getting old or falling ill. (Their excuses: they had no spare room; they could not afford to keep them; they would not pay for 'idleness'.) If they were fortunate, servants found a home with friends or relations, handing over any savings they had stashed away to pay for their keep. But if they had no-one to turn to, then they had to beg for charity from churches or from women's clubs set up to help the needy. If no help came, their only refuge was the workhouse: a grim, prison-like institution, and a most miserable place to end their days.

A workhouse meal

Gruel again!

Susan counts her blessings

'A servant should ... find comfort in the fact that [s]he is spared the responsibilities and vexations which attach themselves to the higher spheres of society.'

The Dictionary of Daily Wants, 1858–1859

CHAPTER ONE

'DOMESTICS NO LONGER KNOW THEIR PLACE'[1]

The year is 1851; Queen Victoria and her clever, handsome husband, Prince Albert, are at the peak of their royal prestige and popularity. Britain proudly claims to be 'the workshop of the world', and controls a mighty empire 'on which the sun never sets'.[2] In London, crowds flock to admire the most up-to-date British art, science, technology, industries and inventions, all grandly displayed in a Great Exhibition.

1. *Mrs Beeton*, Book of Household Management, *1861*.
2. *That is to say, it stretched right round the world, so that some part of it was always in daylight.*

 13

faces in the crowd

Now, travel back in time to imagine that you are strolling through the streets of London with the crowds heading for that Exhibition, or visiting another fine Victorian city, such as Manchester, Glasgow or Liverpool. Or perhaps you're arriving – by horse-drawn coach or the exciting new steam railway – at a busy country town on market day. As you gaze at the men, women and children around you, it's clear that their lives and lifestyles are not all the same.

Some Victorians are clearly rich: well fed, well dressed, confident and commanding. Others – thin, weak, pale and dressed in rags – are pitifully poor. Some are obviously tradesmen – such as shopkeepers in their long aprons, or chimney sweeps carrying bundles of sooty brushes. There are beggars, flower sellers, uniformed police and wandering musicians. But the two most important – and largest – groups of workers in Britain in 1851 are nowhere to be seen. They are busy – out in the fields, or shut away indoors. Who are they?

'DOMESTICS NO LONGER KNOW THEIR PLACE'

According to the newly completed national census[1] of 1851, Britain's most numerous workers are farm labourers, who produce the nation's food – and domestic servants: cooks, cleaners, children's carers and many more household helpers who live and work in other families' homes.

In 1851 there are almost 1.8 million farm workers and nearly 1.04 million household servants in England, Scotland and Wales, out of a total adult population of around 15.75 million. That's not counting thousands more domestic servants working on farms. This means that one out of every 14 or 15 people of working age (over 10 years old, in Victorian times) is a servant.

> And don't forget – most of us servants are women!

In 1851, there are over 900,000 female domestic servants – but only around 130,000 male ones.

1. *official population count.*

15

'Numerous and universal'

Seen or unseen, domestic servants were everywhere in Victorian times. By 1871 an astonishing one in eight of all adult women in England and Wales was a household servant, cleaner or washerwoman – a total of 1,204,477 busy – and often exhausted – females.

In 1871 there were also 124,333 male household servants – though their numbers were falling fast, as working men sought better-paid, more independent employment in mines, iron foundries, railways, dockyards and factories.

No wonder one nineteenth-century book offering advice to servants could claim that:

'No relations in society are so numerous and universal as those of Masters and Servants.'

S. and S. Adams, The Complete Servant, *1825*

A few nineteenth-century writers argued that servanthood must be a system designed by God – and quoted the Bible to prove it:

> 'The various stations of life are appointed by that Supreme Being who is the giver of all goodness.'

> 'The Lord blesses the honest and upright servant.'

from The House Servant's Directory, *1827*

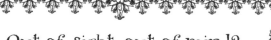

Out of sight, out of mind?

Many servants are not seen because they work 'below stairs' in dark, damp kitchens, basements and corridors, where rich home-owners never venture, or else because they get up extremely early to clean elegant rooms before the 'gentry' are out of bed.

But a few employers claim to find the mere sight of servants offensive: at Crewe Hall in Cheshire, it is said that no housemaids are ever to be seen, except at chapel.

The 'servant question'

God-given or not, few Victorian families looked on their domestic servants as real-life 'godsends'. In fact, they often complained about them. Here is Mrs Beeton, reporting fashionable conversations, in 1861:

'It is another conviction of "Society"[1] that the race of good servants has died out, at least in England ... that there is neither honesty, conscientiousness, nor the careful and industrious habits which distinguished the servants of our grandmothers and great-grandmothers; that domestics no longer know their place.'

Had Victorian servants really grown slack, lazy and rude? Were they no longer keeping to their 'God-given' place as meek, dutiful household members? Had they forgotten to feel sorry for the poor, and relieved (see page 12) that they did not have fine houses and vast landed estates to manage, or powerful positions in government, the Church, and/or fashionable society? Almost certainly not!

1. *people who claimed to belong to the 'better' and/or richer classes.*

Servants never had been as meek – or as clean or as careful – as Victorian employers liked to think. Over 100 years before Mrs Beeton, Irish author Jonathan Swift wrote a satirical list of 'Instructions for Servants' (in 1745). It was his way of complaining about the men and women who worked for him:

'When you have done a fault, be always pert [impertinent] and insolent, and behave yourself as if you were the injured person; this will immediately put your master or lady off their mettle [strong feelings].'

'Never wear socks when you wait at meals...because most young ladies like the smell of a young man's toes.'

'Leave a pail of dirty water with a mop in it, a coal-box, a broom, a chamber-pot and other such unsightly things...upon the darkest part of the back stairs, that they may not be seen; and if people break their shins by trampling on [tripping over] them, it is their own fault.'

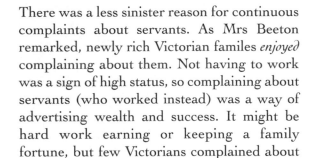

A terrible, tragic revenge

A few servants went much further than Swift's insolent, smelly, careless employees. In 1800 a young, inexperienced nursemaid, Anne Mead, was accused of poisoning Charles Proctor, her employer's baby. Anne gave the baby arsenic because her mistress had called her 'a dirty slut' for not changing his nappy – and was 'resolved to spite' her employer.

Anne was hanged, aged 16.

There was a less sinister reason for continuous complaints about servants. As Mrs Beeton remarked, newly rich Victorian familes *enjoyed* complaining about them. Not having to work was a sign of high status, so complaining about servants (who worked instead) was a way of advertising wealth and success. It might be hard work earning or keeping a family fortune, but few Victorians complained about having wealth, position and power.

In the early years of Victoria's reign new industries – and new industrial towns – were growing fast. By 1851, for the first time ever, over half the population of England lived in a city or town, along with their servants. Books like Mrs Beeton's were aimed at the newly rich, anxious, hopeful, town-dwelling middle classes – and also at rich industrialists, bankers and businessmen who built fine new houses in the country. None had been brought up in 'polite society', surrounded by servants. They wanted to know how to manage them.

'Dependent on servants'[1]

Whatever the Victorians said about their servants, they could not have survived without them. All prosperous Victorian families – one household in four – had at least one servant. By around 1890, almost half of those servants worked alone, or with just one colleague. By contrast, rich people might have up to 50 servants, all living and working in one huge household. The Duke of Westminster in the 1890s had over 300.

1. *Mrs Beeton. She wrote: 'The sensible master and mistress know that…they are dependent on their servants for very many of the comforts of life.'*

Hard-working, well-trained domestic help was essential for any Victorian family that aimed to be elegant, refined, civilised, genteel – or simply to live in a large, clean, comfortable home and eat regular, pleasant meals. Victorian cooking and cleaning equipment was slow, heavy and cumbersome; housework was exhausting and time-consuming. Hardly any homes had electricity, and only a few had gas, except for lighting. Clean piped water and flush lavatories were not widespread – even among servant-owning classes – until late Victorian times.

Even in grand stately homes, cooking was done on dusty, unreliable coal-burning ranges or on huge revolving spits set in cavernous chimneys. Rooms were heated by wood or coal fires that needed cleaning and re-laying every day. After dark, light came from oil lamps that needed regular fillling and trimming. There were no fridges, freezers or microwaves. Washing, even babies' nappies, was done by hand (laundrywomen were famous for their strong arms) and hung outside to dry. As another Victorian writer observed:

'Without the constant co-operation of well-trained servants, domestic machinery [i.e. the well-run house] is completely thrown out of gear.'

from The Servant's Practical Guide, *1880*

The cost of (genteel) living

In the 1880s, British farmers – and many landowners – faced an economic crisis. Food prices and the value of land fell sharply. But the cost of housing, schooling and servants' wages did not; in fact, servants' wages rose as men and women began to find alternative employment. So did the tax that the government charged families who employed men servants (women were tax-free). In 1861, Mrs Beeton calculated that a family earning £750 a year (equivalent to around £60,000 today) could afford to employ a cook, a housemaid, a nursemaid and a boy (to do odd jobs, run errands and clean boots and shoes). By 1906, when a new edition of Beeton's book was published, the same family could only afford a cook and a housemaid. As servants became more expensive, people became more critical of them, and more demanding.

Why be a servant?

From 1851 until the end of Victoria's reign in 1901, domestic service was the choice of around 40 per cent of the women who worked in Britain. Servants faced long hours, hard work, low pay, few holidays, loss of freedom, loneliness, bullying, uncomfortable uniforms, constant supervision and frequent criticism. So why did so many young Victorians choose to become servants?

What are the rewards?

• A roof over your head (probably in a garret)

Yes, ma'am...
Very good, ma'am...
At once, ma'am...

• Clothes (a uniform that tells *everyone* what you are)

• Food and drink (often other people's leftovers)

• Wages (and tips, if you're lucky)

- Perks (e.g. dripping, if you're the cook)

- Christmas presents (don't get too excited – it'll be a new apron, or cloth to make yourself a new uniform)

- The company of other servants (but will you like them?)

- A splendid house to work in (perhaps)

SERVANTS' ENTRANCE ROUND THE BACK

- Reflected glory from your rich employers (who may never so much as look at you)

- Time off (one Sunday afternoon every six weeks – let's hope the weather's nice)

Never darken my door again!

- Job security (you hope).

And what are the alternatives?

Early Victorian

- Factory hand (working with dangerous machinery)

Aaargh!

- Coal mine (dirt, dust, risk of explosions)

- Farm labourer (mud, back-breaking toil)

- At home, looking after younger siblings (dirt, noise, squabbling)

- Seamstress (hard on the eyes)

- Flower seller (out in all weathers, splashed with mud and horse manure)

- Criminal gang (think *Oliver Twist*).

Late Victorian

- Shop assistant

- Waitress or barmaid

- Lace-maker

- Straw-plaiter (for making hats)

And, only if you're educated:

- Clerk
- Typist
- Junior civil servant
- Nurse
- Schoolteacher.

What can you tell me about the British Empire?

Don't fancy any of those?

Then your choices are very limited:

- Workhouse
- Orphanage
- Begging
- Sent overseas (to Australia or Canada).

His Lordship will not be kept waiting

'As long as the rich pay for what they desire, they have every right to please themselves.'

From The Ladies' Maid, *1838*

CHAPTER TWO

THE BEST CIRCLES

As Mrs Beeton observed in 1861: 'There are few families of respectability, from the shopkeeper in the next street to the nobleman whose mansion dignifies the next square, which do not contain among their dependents attached and useful servants.' This was true, although real-life Victorian employers complained that not all servants were as 'attached' (loyal) or 'useful' as Mrs Beeton might hope them to be. As one Victorian writer sweepingly declared: 'Servants as a class are not to be trusted' – though he did admit that few employers would like to work as servants themselves. Having always to obey orders was extremely disagreeable:

'However comfortable a servant may be made, still there is the constant subjection to the caprices[1] of a fellow being.'

J. H. Walsh, A Manual of Domestic Economy, 1857

Brrring!

Sometimes the mistress's caprices gives me 'eadache.

1. *changing wishes.*

false impressions?

Today, thanks to films, TV costume dramas, the heritage industry and nostalgic novels (such as those by P. G. Wodehouse), the term 'domestic servant' conjures up a fantastic – and fanciful – vanished Victorian community. It's peopled by imperturbable butlers, efficient housekeepers, prim governesses, pretty, giggling housemaids and dashing, liveried[1] footmen, along with gnarled old gardeners and cheeky young errand-boys. All live, work, flirt, quarrel, gossip and intrigue in their own fascinating world 'below stairs'.

In fact, this 'world of servants' is mostly a mirage. Only a quarter of Victorian families had servants, and, among them, only around a third employed more than one full-time domestic worker. The typical Victorian servant lived and worked alone. You can read more about these solitary servants' experiences in Chapter 5. Let's look now at what life was like for the minority of servants, who lived and worked surrounded by other 'domestics' in a large and busy household.

1. *smartly uniformed.*

Maid – or horse?

In 1857, J. H. Walsh, author of *A Manual of Domestic Economy*, suggested the number of servants (and horses!) suitable for families with different levels of income. He ignored the super-rich, beginning with families receiving £1,500 a year – still a considerable income:

• **£1,500 (= £120,000 today): Seven servants, at least two horses and a coach**
Butler, coachman or groom,[1] housemaid (or two), cook, lady's maid or nursemaid (or both).

• **£500 (= £40,000 today): Three servants, plus a horse and carriage**
Manservant or parlourmaid, housemaid, cook. However, 'If the family is a large one, a young ladies' maid must be kept for the purpose of making their dresses at home, and in that case a horse cannot be afforded.'

• **£250 (= £20,000 today): One and a half servants**
A maid-of-all-work 'assisted sometimes by a girl…or by the younger members of the family'.

• **£100 (= £10,000 today): Half a servant**
'Barely sufficient' to provide housing, food and clothes for a family. 'No servant can be kept, or …only such a young girl as it is quite useless here to allude to.'[2]

1. *almost certainly from the workhouse (see page 11).*
2. *allude to: mention; this girl too would be from the workhouse.*

Seven full-time servants, as recommended opposite, seems a large staff to look after one married couple and their children (up to six children was the Victorian average). Yet they fade into insignificance when compared with the 300-plus servants who worked in 1839 at Woburn Abbey, the ancient stately home of the Dukes of Bedford.

But among the 'best circles' – as the Victorians called the topmost ranks of society – keeping servants, and giving them orders, was not done for 'any pleasure'. Instead, as the author of *The Ladies' Maid* (1838) helpfully explained:

> 'A rich lady has a great many servants...
> because she wants to save her own time and
> thoughts by hiring other people to do, without
> any care of hers, what she likes to have done.'

And, of course, the growing numbers of middle-class women tried to copy her:

> 'Wives and daughters at home[1] now do less
> domestic work than their predecessors; hence
> the excessive demand for female servants...'

Official government report on the 1871 census.

1. that is, those who can afford not to go out to work.

female servants

Housekeeper
Stillroom Maid

Governess

Cook
Kitchen Maid
Tweeny
Scullion

Lady's Maid
Young Ladies' Maid

Head Nurse
Second Nurse
Nurserymaid

Dairymaid

**Upper
Housemaid**
Under
Housemaid
Chambermaid

**Upper
Laundrymaid**
Under
Laundrymaid

Male servants

Land Steward   House Steward
Steward's room boy

Chef

Butler
Under Butler

Valet

Head Gamekeeper
Under Gamekeepers

Head Gardener
Under Gardeners

Coachman
Lady's Coachman
Groom
Stable Boy

Footman
Lady's Footman
Under Footman
Page (Errand Boy)

Hall Porter

Domestic duties

Just what did dukes, duchesses and others in the best circles (or hoping to join them) 'like to have done' around their homes? What duties did they expect their households full of servants to perform? The short answer is 'almost everything', from intimate personal services (Lord Byron's valet routinely administered enemas to his master) to running vast agricultural estates or entertaining royalty. From the lowliest 'scullion' or 'tweeny' to the grandest 'groom of the chamber', each separate servant had his or her own special task to do – and their own special place in the pecking order.

But what did these people actually do? What were their job descriptions?

So you wish to obtain a situation here? We'll see.

Situations vacant: female

• Housekeeper

Experienced manager required, to keep a huge household running smoothly. Can you hire and fire servants and organise their work? Can you order groceries for several hundred people, together with all other domestic supplies, from coal to soap and candles? Can you plan cooking, cleaning, house decoration and repairs, mending and laundry? Can you make fancy preserves, sweetmeats, perfumes, home remedies, wine from wild flowers, or vinegar 'from the refuse of bee-hives'? Do you know how to roast, grind, brew and serve that expensive imported luxury, coffee?

Can you keep accounts? Can you soothe a worried mistress? Calm a temperamental chef? Or battle with a drunken butler?

Only steady, tactful, diligent and devoted middle-aged women (unmarried or widowed) need apply.

That's me!

• Governess

You're refined, well educated, nicely spoken and have genteel manners. You speak French (perhaps you *are* French), play the piano, and sew delicate embroideries. Preferably, you sketch or paint. You read and recite poetry. You're young and probably untrained, but you come from a middle-class family, or above. It helps if you like children, but (surprisingly) that's not essential – even though you'll spend almost all your time with them.

• Lady's maid

Are you pretty? And clever? And charming? And discreet? Energetic, always willing to help, and pleasant company? Are you neat and tidy, patient and good-tempered? Are you stylish? And do you follow fashion? Being a lady's maid sounds fun – but remember, you'll spend all day and half the night making someone else look beautiful. And you must always look worse-dressed and less attractive than her.

Only young women need apply. Old ladies' maids are NOT wanted.

> Impudence! I was reckoned a head-turner in my day, I can tell you.

• **Head nurse**
You'll have their lives in your hands – literally!
It will be your job to care for all the babies born
to 'your' rich or noble family, until they are
teenagers. You'll do everything from feeding
them and singing lullabies to nursing them
through childhood illnesses and taking them to
parties. You'll also make them say their prayers
– and take cold baths every morning.
(Victorians believe that this is a good way to
make children grow strong and healthy.)
Expect hard work, sleepless nights,
busy, anxious days – and, if you're
lucky, a lot of love in return.
Your charges will spend
more time with you than
with their mother.

• **Second nurse**
Have you worked
as a nurserymaid?
Yes? Then you'll have
learned a lot on the
job. Now you'll be
looking for promotion
and more responsibility.
It's likely that you'll do
most of the 'hands-on'
baby care, while the
head nurse supervises.
Here's a good chance to
extend your skills, and
get more experience.

• Nurserymaid

You're probably still a child yourself: many nursemaids start work soon after their tenth birthday. But, however hard it is, you must forget all ideas of playing. This job will be hard – and dirty and smelly and tiring. Expect lots of used nappies, soiled clothes, messy dishes, muddy nursery floors and children's sticky fingers to wash. It will also be your task to carry (heavy!) babies and toddlers for their daily 'walk' in the fresh air – unless your employer has one of those newfangled perambulators (folding buggies have not yet been dreamed of).

• Upper housemaid

Are you a heavy sleeper who finds it hard to get up in the morning? Then this job's not for you! As head housemaid, leading a hard-working team of cleaners, polishers, bed-makers, fire-lighters and carriers of coal, water and smelly slops, you have to set an example. Be up and dressed by 5.00 a.m. at the very latest – and prepare to work all day long.

They don't have many secrets from me, you know.

• Under housemaid

Only apply for this job if you're young, strong – and can't find anything better. The work's hard, dirty and boring – and you *always* have to do as you're told. You even have to work during your 'rest' time (a couple of hours to sit down, in the afternoon). That's when you're meant to do the mending: patching and stitching work clothes, sheets, towels and tablecloths.

• Kitchen maid

Hold out your hands! Let's look at them! Are they really, really clean? And are your nails clean too – trimmed short, and scrubbed – and is your hair tied back neatly? You'll be helping Chef to prepare important meals, and he's very particular. You'll cook everyday food for the servants, as well – and light the cooking fires or range, and clean the kitchen!

Home, home on the range...

• **Upper laundrymaid**
Do you know how to handle a dolly,[1] or get the best out of blue?[2] Can you cope with a copper?[3] Manage a mangle?[4] Are you practised with a possing stick?[5] Of course, you'll be big and brawny – and you'll drink beer for breakfast. No wonder, since you'll often start work at 3.00 a.m. on Mondays (washdays) and won't finish until midnight!

• **Under laundrymaid**
You'll help the chief laundrymaid – and your work will be just as heavy and exhausting as hers. But you might find some compensations. The hot, steamy air of the washhouse will make your cheeks prettily pink and your hair nicely wavy. And you'll have plenty of visitors to your washhouse; they'll come to get warm on cold mornings – and to admire you. Young laundrymaids are famous for attracting the boys!

• **Dairymaid**
Do you care for cows? Can you churn butter, press cheese, collect eggs – and kill and pluck

1. dolly: wooden stick with four prongs at the end, used to pound and swirl clothes being washed.
2. blue: bright blue dye. Small quantities were added to rinsing water and made white washing look brighter.
3. copper: huge copper cauldron, with a coal fire at the base, used to heat water or boil dirty clothes.
4. mangle: a pair of heavy rollers with a handle attached. Turned by hand, this spun the rollers to squeeze water out of wet washing.
5. possing stick: a copper cup on a wooden pole. It was pressed up and down on wet washing to try to remove stains by suction.

turkeys, geese and chickens? Yes? Then this may be the job for you – so long as you can bear to work in a damp, cold, dark dairy, with water running over the floor to cool it all year round.

• **Stillroom maid**
Can you be trusted with household stores, preserves and medicines? Are you tidy, methodical and willing to learn? You'll be assistant – and personal servant – to the housekeeper herself. You'll help make jams and remedies, check stock in the store-room, wash up the noble family's best china, and wait on the housekeeper at table. She'll demand total obedience, but can teach you many useful skills.

• **Tweeny**
Neither one nor the other: that's you, if you become a 'tweeny', or in-between maid. You'll work as an extra pair of hands, helping the housemaids and the kitchen maid, wherever you're wanted.

• **Scullion (or scullery maid)**
There probably are worse jobs for servants to do, but it's not easy to think of them. You'll be washing greasy plates, bowls and dishes, lighting sooty fires, peeling muddy vegetables, running errands for the cook, and scrubbing kitchen tables, walls and floors. You'll have no kitchen machines or detergents to help you – and no hot water on tap. Instead, you'll rely on 'elbow grease' and harsh soap or soda, which will make your hands red and raw.

RULES

for Victorian servants
at Chirk Castle, Wales

Each servant must:

- Remove his hat when entering •
- Sit at his proper place[1] •
- Keep clean •
- Wait his turn for drink •
- Work diligently •
- Shut all doors after him •

Each servant must NOT:

- Swear • Tell tales •
- Speak disrespectfully •
- Start a quarrel •
- Waste food or drink •
- Meddle with any other servant's work (unless asked to help) •

1. *Servants were seated and served in order of rank.*

Situations vacant: Male

• Land steward

Well educated, businesslike, with a working knowledge of the law, you'll be His Lordship's right-hand man. You'll collect all the rents from his tenants, manage his fields and farms, his livestock, his haymaking and his harvest. You'll organise maintenance and repairs of all his farm buildings, and all the roads, gates and fences around his estate. You'll also supervise all the 'outdoor' servants – from gardeners to hired hands. You must have plenty of farming experience – ideally, you'll have been born and bred on the land and, like His Lordship, will come from a noble, or at least a 'gentleman's' family.

•House steward

His Lordship is pleased to leave the paperwork to me.

Only excellent organisers with first-class business, legal and people skills need apply. Your task will be to manage the smooth running of the entire household and all its servants. You'll work closely with the housekeeper, the land steward and the butler. But you'll be in overall control, so, if anything goes wrong, be prepared to take the blame.

• Chef

Oh la la! Ideally you'll be French – talented, charming, clever and creative. Or you might be Italian – foreign cookery is fashionable among rich Victorians. It won't matter too much if you lose your temper, swear or throw dishes around, so long as you produce fantastic food – and plenty of it – for four meals every day, and serve splendid dishes to impress guests when they visit.

Less wealthy households will probably prefer a female cook. She'll be cheaper to employ (women's wages are *always* lower) but no less talented or hard-working.

• Butler

Are you calm, capable, unflappable? Good at many different tasks, from supervising breakfast to washing dozens of glasses and cleaning all your employer's silver candlesticks, plates and dishes? (You'll have to sleep beside them too, to keep them safe from burglars.) Are you courteous and dignified? (You'll have to receive visitors to the house.) A good judge of beer

You rang, sir?

and wine? (You'll be in charge of his lordship's cellar.) Pleasant yet firm? You'll have to preside in the servants' hall, where all the junior staff take their meals.

•Valet

A 'gentleman's gentleman', that's what you'll be – even though you come from a very ordinary family. (Personal services are tasks for 'the lower orders', in most Victorians' eyes.) Do you have what it takes to bathe, shave and dress your master, care for his clothes, pack his luggage, wind his watch, trim his hair and generally look after him? One word of advice: in such a confidential position, you're bound to overhear many secrets – sweet and shocking. Forget them all. Be discreet! Above all, don't gossip.

• Coachman

Of course, you'll be a safe driver, with an expert knowledge of horses. Of course, you'll need to know how to keep your employer's coaches and carriages clean, and arrange for any repairs to be completed straight away. But you'll also have to look smart – yes, you'll wear the traditional three-cornered hat! – as you drive your employers through the busy streets and town squares. They – and you – will be on public display.

•Footman

Here's another job where looks really matter. In fact, you'll earn more if you are young, tall and handsome. Try to find a friend of the same height and build to work alongside you. Employers like 'matching pairs' of footmen to run behind their coach, or open their front door to visitors. You'll also have to wait at table (do you have a steady hand?), clean the knives,[1] polish the furniture, dust the mirrors and oil paintings, trim the lamps, and much, much more.

One final question. Roll up your trouser-legs. Let me see: do you have well-developed calves and shapely ankles? Remember, your legs will be on show – you'll have to wear a striped waistcoat, a powdered wig, silk stockings and knee-breeches!

• Under footman

Smart, quick and keen to impress? Don't mind the thought of a lifetime at everyone's beck and call? If you want to train as a footman, start as a boy – 10 or 12 years old is not too young.

1. *Victorian knives had iron blades which quickly went rusty.*

• Groom
Only men with horse sense need apply for this vacancy. It will be your job to feed, clean and train all your employer's horses – and exercise them, and muck out their stables, and nurse them when they fall sick. You'll have to clean and mend their harness too, and wash and polish the coaches. All day long you'll live among horses – and at night you'll sleep in the hayloft above their stables.

• Head gamekeeper
Wild about wildlife? Handy with a gun? Got strong legs and a tough constitution? (You'll have to walk miles over moorland, often in the pouring rain.) Then His Lordship needs a man like you to manage the shooting on his estate, and organise the under gamekeepers and beaters. It's a strange job, spending time and tender care rearing creatures to be killed for fun. Deer, grouse, pheasant and partridge are the favourite targets. Bring your own dog.

• Head gardener
You'll need green fingers to succeed as gardener or under gardener – and a healthy back for digging flowerbeds, and strong arms for lifting heavy loads. You'll have to grow flowers, trees, fruit and vegetables, plus exotic rarities in the estate greenhouses; pineapples are surprisingly popular.

Overcrowded!

'Besides the ordinary establishment of servants, noblemen and gentlemen of superior fortune employ... BAILIFFS, WOODWARDS...PARK-KEEPERS, HUNTSMEN, WHIPPERS-IN, RACING GROOM, JOCKEYS and others of inferior capacities: also MEN-COOKS, GROOM OF THE CHAMBERS, PAGE, LADY's COACHMAN, POSTILLION AND FOOTMAN, SEAMSTRESS, SECOND LADY'S MAID, CHAMBER-MAIDS, BOY FOR THE STEWARD'S ROOM, ANOTHER FOR THE HALL, and various other servants.'

S. and S. Adams, The Complete Servant, *1825*

Did splendid surroundings and constant companionship make for better working conditions, or happier relations with employers? Not always. Some servants found life in a large, busy household altogether too exhausting. Others did not like being given orders by senior servants, or were tormented by their fellow workers.

For some, it was all a bit too much...

Content to serve

'I felt unequal to being anything like an "upper"... [I'd] always been "under", and never wishing to think myself as highest or lowest servant in the house, it was awkward and contrary.'

Letter from servant Hannah Cullwick, after taking a job as an 'upper' servant (a cook) in a house with several other servants, 1868

First sent to work aged 8, and orphaned at 14, Victorian servant Hannah Cullwick (pictured on page 88) led an extraordinary life. Tall, strong, good-looking, determined and very independent-minded, she worked in several large houses before deciding that she would prefer a career as a solitary maid-of-all-work. Unlike most other servants, she kept a diary, recording her thoughts and feelings as well as her exhausting daily routine. Her chores ranged from sweeping chimneys (by climbing them) to cleaning lavatories and scrubbing rat-infested sculleries. The dirtier the job, the more she enjoyed it – or so she claimed. Strangest of all, tough, grimy, working-class Hannah secretly wed a delicate, mild-mannered, upper-middle-class writer and lawyer, Arthur Munby. He was fascinated by strong working women – and was delighted when Hannah picked him up in her arms or nursed him on her lap like a baby. They were very happily married for over 40 years.

Cook ruled her domain with a rod of iron

'The presidency of the kitchen [is] a situation
of great trust and responsibility.'

*Robert Roberts, The House Servants'
Directory, 1826*

CHAPTER THREE

DINNER IS SERVED

Who was the most important servant in a Victorian household? The steward, the housekeeper and the butler were usually the highest-ranking, but in many ways the cook or chef was the most valued and most powerful. He – or she – deserves a special chapter.

Most cooks were women, but the greatest, most fashionable families, including Queen Victoria's, employed foreign male chefs. Traditionally these were French, highly trained, highly skilled and highly paid. They were also status symbols. The more foreign chefs, or French-trained English male cooks, that worked in any household, the more impressive it appeared.

Many Victorian employers were willing to turn a blind eye to bad temper, eccentricity or even drunkenness in the kitchen, so long as their chef dished up delicacies to delight dinner guests. Only a few traditionalists protested:

'An English girl properly instructed can equal the best foreign gentleman in everything except impudence and extravagance, and send up a delicious dinner with half the usual expense and trouble.'

Dr Kitchener, c.1820

Cooking for a large household demanded phenomenal organisational skills, as well as good taste and culinary talent. Wealthy Victorian families liked to entertain guests to dinners, soirées (evening parties), receptions and balls at least once a month. Victorian cookbooks include dinner and supper menus listing 30 or 40 dishes, all elaborately decorated. Grand dinners – like those served in royal palaces – might have 14 separate courses. It was the cook's task to produce all these – perfectly cooked, hot or chilled as required, on time, and in good order.

The perks of the job

Keeping a cook was not cheap. In 1862, a top female cook in Edinburgh earned about £50 per year (= £40,000 today) plus free board and lodging. A top male chef could earn twice as much or more, and London rates for men and women were higher still. An ordinary cook in a middle-class provincial family was much less expensive: she might earn only £15 (£12,000) per year. In 1898, Queen Victoria's celebrity chef was paid a staggering £400 (= almost £200,000 today), but he was exceptional.

Money was not everything. A cook or chef would also expect to receive perquisites (leftovers or by-products) from the job, such as rabbit skins, dripping and old tea leaves; all could be sold to dealers who called at the house to collect them. Stale food was sold as pigswill; rags and bones went to make paper and glue. The cook would also expect commission (gifts of money or produce) from local traders. This was meant to show thanks to regular customers for their purchases, but often it was more like blackmail. A cook might threaten to buy the vast quantities of food needed for a wealthy household from a different supplier, if commission was not sufficiently generous.

Help at hand

A cook's wages and perquisites were not the only expense for employers; few cooks worked alone. In large households they had kitchen maids, tweenies and scullery maids to help them; even in small households there was usually one other maid employed. These women (junior kitchen workers were almost always female) did all the hardest, dirtiest kitchen jobs, from scrubbing greasy pots and pans to chopping onions and gutting rabbits, leaving the cook or chef free to concentrate on creative cuisine.

A kitchen maid's day

5.00 a.m. Get up, wash in cold water, get dressed. Tiptoe silently downstairs in stockinged feet – but don't tread on the black beetles that infest most Victorian kitchens (along with mice, cockroaches, fleas and crickets).

5.30 a.m. Collect beetle traps (set the previous night) and kill the beetles in them. Clean and 'blacklead' kitchen range; light kitchen fire.

6.00 a.m. Scrub kitchen tables and floor.

7.00 a.m. Wake cook and senior kitchen servants with a cup of tea.

7.30 a.m. Help make servants' breakfast.

8.00 a.m. Eat breakfast.

8.30 – 10.30 a.m. Prepare vegetables. All through the day, make sure kitchen range is filled with coal and burning brightly – or else soot and ashes will drop into the food.

10.30 a.m. – 11.00 a.m. Help make servants' lunch.

11.00 a.m. Eat lunch.

11.30 a.m. – 1.00 p.m. Rest period: mend aprons, stockings, caps.

1.00 – 4.30 p.m. Help cook make sauces (one per dish – all different!).

4.30 p.m. Help make servants' tea.

5.00 p.m. Eat tea

5.30 – 8.30 p.m. Cook now drunk. Panic! Help senior kitchen maids to finish cooking important main meal for employers.

8.30 – 9.00 p.m. Help make servants' supper.

9.00 p.m. Eat supper.

9.30 p.m. Set traps to catch black beetles.

10.00 p.m. Go to bed – exhausted!

foods for a buffet supper

'Beef, ham and tongue sandwiches, lobster and oyster patties, sausage rolls, meat rolls, lobster salad, dishes of fowl, the latter all cut up; dishes of sliced ham, sliced tongue, sliced beef and galantines of veal; various jellies, blancmanges and creams; custards in glasses; compotes of fruit; tartlets of jam, and several dishes of small fancy pastry; dishes of fresh fruit, bonbons, sweetmeats, two or three sponge cakes, a few plates of biscuits, and the buffet [side-table] ornamented with vases of fresh or artificial flowers.'

Mrs Beeton, 1861

fact and fantasy

In Victorian times, as today, cookery books dealt in dreams and fantasies. Many were written for wealthy women – who did not know how to cook – wanting to learn how to order nice (and fashionable) meals from their servants. Few real-life cooks managed to live up to cookery writers' standards of elaborate perfection. But some obviously tried. Queen Victoria's kitchens at Windsor Castle were described as being 'like a chapel', where chefs, assistant cooks and kitchen maids worked in complete silence, to aid their 'intense concentration'.[1]

Just occasionally, diaries written by hostesses – and by servants – record actual meals cooked and eaten by real-life Victorian people.

The list opposite shows a real day's meals cooked for one old lady and her daughter in 1837, together with their servants' meals, recorded a few days earlier. The old lady employed three female servants and one man. At the time these menus were recorded, she and her daughter had no guests, and so did not demand as much cooking from their servants as usual.

The whole household ate good plain food – and plenty of it. Servants often ate at different times from their employers. This left them free to finalise cooking, wait at table, and clear away the dishes.

1. The Queen also employed a team of Indian servants to kill sheep and chickens according to their own religious traditions, and to roast and grind oriental spices. Presumably, the Empress of India – or her guests – had a liking for 'authentic' curries.

A day's meals

Employers

Breakfast 9.00 a.m. Hot rolls, toast, fancy bread, plain bread, butter, tea or chocolate.

Lunch 1.00 p.m. Cold meat, vegetables.

Dinner 6.00 p.m. Fried sole with sauce, leg of mutton, dish of beef, young chickens, potatoes, broccoli, rice, rhubarb tart, tapioca pudding, cheese, butter.

Evening meal 8.00 p.m. Bread, butter, toast, tea.

Servants

Breakfast 8.00 a.m. Bread, butter, toast. Servants had to pay for their own tea and sugar if required; otherwise there was ale to drink.

Dinner around 1.00 p.m. Cold beef, broccoli, potatoes, damson pie.

Tea 4.00 p.m. Bread, butter, sometimes cake.

Supper 9.00 p.m. Cold beef, damson pie (leftovers from lunch, presumably).

Not all servants were so well cared for:

'It is usual for servants to have lunch, either bread and cheese or a piece of cake, about eleven o'clock; but they should not be allowed to sit down to it.'

K. Mellish, Cookery and Domestic Management, *1901*

On some Yorkshire farms, servants did not even eat from plates, but from hollows carved into the kitchen table. Each farmhand had his own knife and spoon. At the end of the meal, the table was scrubbed with hot water or rubbed dry with straw.

Kitchen or laboratory?

Victorians loved the latest gadgets. In his guide to setting up and running *The Gentleman's House* (1864), Robert Kerr approvingly remarked that the latest country-house kitchens had 'the character of a complicated laboratory'. To us, their coal-fired ranges, Dutch ovens, roasting jacks, stewing stoves, turnspits, tea urns, hotplates and heating cupboards look ancient, inefficient and a nightmare to keep clean, but they were once the latest technology. Proud owners even had them photographed – another Victorian invention!

But kitchens in poor homes could be damp, windowless places with greasy, bloodstained work surfaces – literally places of blood, sweat and toil.

Changing food fashions

Grand Victorian families found many ways of making more work for servants. Afternoon tea is said to have been invented around the start of Victoria's reign by Anna, Duchess of Bedford, at Woburn, a magnificent stately home in south-east England. She ordered her servants there to bring tea and cakes halfway between luncheon at 1.00 p.m. and dinner at 8.00 p.m., to combat 'a sinking feeling'.

Other food fashions took up much more time and trouble, especially for cooks (who had to time their meals to perfection) and footmen (who waited at table). In the early 19th century, fashionable people dined *à la française* (in the French manner). They sat around a table spread with many different dishes, and helped each other to portions of those they wished to eat. At the same time the host and hostess, sitting at opposite ends of the table, carved the main roast meats and offered slices to their guests. Servants took away empty dishes and replaced them with new ones. Eating a grand dinner this way took a long time, but was friendly and convivial.

Around 1850, a new way of eating became popular. Known as dining *à la russe* (in the Russian manner), it was similar to a very formal restaurant meal today. Guests were led to table by their host and hostess, sat down, and then waited for servants to bring several separate courses one at a time and offer them portions. Instead of one or two servants to serve dinner *à la française*, a whole troop of footmen had to be on duty to serve a meal *à la russe*. Ideally, there was one footman per guest – and Victorian dinner parties often had 12 guests and more. If there were not enough menservants in a household, then smart, pretty parlourmaids might serve as well, or else the housekeeper might hire extra footmen for the evening from an employment agency.

Service à la russe
Instructions for servants

- While guests are being seated, a servant outside the dining room brings soup.

- Footman receives soup at the door. Butler serves it out. Footman hands it to diners.

- Butler and footman change diners' plates.

- Footman takes out soup and receives fish at door, while butler hands out wines.

- Butler serves fish. Footman hands it out (plate in one hand, sauce in the other).

- Both change plates.

- Footman brings entrée (a cooked meat dish), while butler hands wine.

- Butler hands entrée. Footman hands vegetables. Both change plates.

And so on until the end of the meal.

Adapted from The Ladies' Guide, *1861*

Susan wrestles with temptation

'Never let idle vanity
Tempt you your ladies' clothes to try
Or in their drawers and cupboards pry.'

Advice to female servants from
The Parish Magazine, 1873

CHAPTER four

PERSONAL SERVICES

A superior servant, that's you! As a valet or lady's maid, you're a well-trained expert with specialist skills. You're better paid than most other servants, and – in grand households – you have juniors to assist you. Like the butler and the governess, you eat apart from the rest of the servants, sharing meals with the housekeeper in her private room. You demand respect, and you don't wear livery – the uniform that shows servants' inferior status. Most important of all, your tasks are personal, intimate, confidential. Can you be trusted?

Are your employer's likes and dislikes, follies and foibles, weirdnesses and weaknesses, safely secret with you?

A gentleman's gentleman

If a man could afford to employ a valet, he was not only rich, but keen to display his wealth by cutting a fine, gentlemanly figure.[1] This meant more than just looking good – though rich Victorians might change their clothes four or five times every day. In the best circles, many different occasions, from horse-riding before breakfast to enjoying a quiet fireside chat late at night, demanded completely different outfits.

Looking after his employer's clothes, by brushing, pressing, airing, polishing, mending, removing stains and storing away neatly, took up a large part of a valet's working day. He also had to choose the most appropriate outfit for his master to wear on each separate occasion, and set it out ready to wear. He had to carry up hot water to his master's bedroom, bring him tea in bed in the mornings, set out

1. *a very Victorian phrase. It means 'showing off with confidence and style'.*

his sponge, soap and toothpaste, help him to take a bath – one elderly Victorian nobleman had to be hoisted into his tub like a sack of coal – shave him, cut his hair, manicure his fingernails, help him put on his clothes, attach his collar,[1] tie his cravat, find his cufflinks, pin on his buttonhole, and check his overall appearance before he left his dressing room to take part in polite society.

At night, the valet waited, and waited, and waited until his master was ready to go to bed, then – having aired his nightgown and warmed his slippers by the fire – he might bring him a bedtime drink.

I've brought your nightcap, sir.

Is he *ever* going to bed? I'm shattered.

1. Victorian shirts had separate, very stiff collars, attached to the neckline with metal and mother-of-pearl studs; shirt cuffs were fastened with metal cufflinks, not buttons.

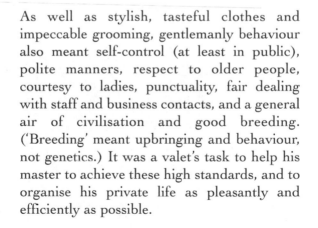

A word of warning

'No master should make a confidant[1] of his
servant, or intrust him with any secret to his
prejudice; this at once gives a servant undue
importance, and leads him to take liberties
which he would not otherwise dare to
contemplate.'

From The Dictionary of Daily Wants, *1858–1859*

1. confidant: a person entrusted with secrets.

As well as stylish, tasteful clothes and
impeccable grooming, gentlemanly behaviour
also meant self-control (at least in public),
polite manners, respect to older people,
courtesy to ladies, punctuality, fair dealing
with staff and business contacts, and a general
air of civilisation and good breeding.
('Breeding' meant upbringing and behaviour,
not genetics.) It was a valet's task to help his
master to achieve these high standards, and to
organise his private life as pleasantly and
efficiently as possible.

Helpless!

Many privileged boys, surrounded by servants since birth, simply did not know how to do everyday tasks without help. A valet offered advice, reminded his master to pay bills, write letters or make duty visits, arranged his travel at home or abroad, purchased his tickets, booked his hotel rooms, packed his luggage and unpacked it at his destination. He accompanied his master on all important journeys, hiring carriages, horses and drivers as needed. If the master fell ill, his valet helped care for him – administering medicines and performing all kinds of intimate body-care tasks if a doctor or trained nurse was not at hand. If his master became drunk, the valet got him home safely.

A good valet did all this tactfully and discreetly, without appearing to give orders to his master. He was smart, neat, well (and softly) spoken:

'[A valet always] has the same noiseless step and perfect sleekness and politeness of manner, the same absolute good temper and gentleness of tone with the same subserviency and perfection of voice...[He is]...agreeable to live with and easy to manage...unobtrusively useful... devoted to...your interest and his...'

Victorian noblewoman Lady Violet Greville

The valet may have helped himself to his master's wine, cigars, writing paper – and socks! – and read his books and newspapers, but, on the whole, he deserved his high wages.

The worm that turned

In 1840, a Swiss valet working in England, François Courvoisier, murdered his master, Lord William Russell, a member of the rich and powerful Duke of Bedford's family. He complained – quite truthfully – that his master was always finding fault with him. One evening, Lord William sent Courvoisier scurrying to and fro on a pointless errand, as a punishment for showing too much initiative. Infuriated, Courvoisier stopped playing the part of a mild-mannered valet, attacked Lord William, and killed him. He was found guilty and hanged.

Airs and graces

In large households where the husband and master employed a valet, his wife and their daughters would each have a maid to look after their personal needs. Always called 'Miss', followed by her surname, as a sign of her professional status, a lady's maid was not like other female servants. Lower-ranking servants were, on the whole, recruited for their strength and endurance; the lady's maid was employed for her refinement, discretion and fashion sense. Ideally she was young, pretty, slender and elegantly dressed, just like a newly married noble lady.

Like a valet, a lady's maid's main tasks were to help her mistress bathe, dress, arrange her hair and apply cosmetics – a shameful secret in Victorian times, when ladies were meant to look 'pure' and 'natural'. Even scent – other than a very faint perfume of violets – was thought unladylike.

Victorian women and girls wore many layers of clothing, and the various garments making up each outfit (skirt, bodice, petticoat, collar, cuffs, etc.) usually had to be carefully buttoned, tied or pinned together each time they were put on. Lace, ribbons, artificial flowers and other trimmings also had to be sewn on before each wearing, then carefully removed and stored away.

Furs were rubbed with bran, shaken, and stored in huge cloth bags; silk shoes were folded in paper. Kid gloves were rubbed with stale bread, then placed in silk cases in a chest of drawers. Tweed coats were covered in powdered clay, then beaten until all traces were removed, before being hung in huge wardrobes. Packing for a visit – on holiday or just to see friends – could be a nightmare:

'To Ramsgate by 12.15 train. 19 large boxes, 17 small, two dogs and six birds [in a cage].'

From the diary of Victorian upper-middle-class lady Marion Sambourne, c.1880

Layers and layers

Here is a list of the plain, everyday garments worn – all at once – by a young upper-class woman in the 1890s. Smart, fashionable dresses, for paying calls on friends or going to evening parties, were much more elaborate.

- Thick woollen combinations[1]
- Frilly white cotton combinations
- Boned corset with suspenders
- Black wool stockings
- Frilly white cotton drawers
- White cotton bodice, frilled and embroidered
- White woollen petticoat
- Long alpaca[2] petticoat
- Flannel (thin wool) blouse
- High, stiff collar
- Silk tie
- Long wool skirt
- Tight leather belt
- Buttoned boots.

1. *vest and knickers in one.*
2. *fine, soft, warm cloth woven from the hair of a South American animal related to the llama.*

Crowning glories

A lady's hair (always long, except in illness, when it was often cropped very short) had to be brushed – 100 times each bedtime was traditional – then, each morning, brushed again and braided, coiled or arranged in elaborate buns, rolls or chignons. Only young, unmarried women went bareheaded, and then only indoors. Married women wore frilled lace caps in the house. Outdoors, all women wore hats, hoods or bonnets. Fashions for these changed from year to year, but were usually elaborate. A top lady's maid had to be a skilled hairdresser, milliner and dressmaker. She also had to know 'the best style to suit her mistress', and was advised (by *Cassell's Household Guide*, 1888) to model her creations on the 'ladies of the royal family of England', who avoid 'all unbecoming exaggerations of fashion, while they adhere sufficiently to the prevailing mode to avoid the opposite error of being eccentric'.

Trusted with treasures

Fine silk dresses, delicate lace and heirloom jewellery were extremely valuable, and ladies' maids were responsible for their care and safe keeping. Washing lace could take days:

1. Remove lace from dress or collar. If new, rub a little clear, sweet oil into it. This helps strengthen the fibres.

2. Lay it flat in a dish of lather skimmed from soap jelly, or sew it to a clean bottle, covered with cloth (this will suport it and help it stay in shape).

3. Pat it gently with the palms of the hands.

4. Rinse – still flat – under running cold water, still patting gently.

5. Rinse again in 'blued' water.[1]

6. Remove excess water by dabbing with a clean, dry cloth.

7. Set out in the sun to dry.

8. When nearly dry, dip lace in starch mixture (previously concocted by lady's maid from rice flour and boiling water, or similar) and leave until partially dry.

1. 'blued' water: water to which a small quantity of blue dye has been added – what would nowadays be called an 'optical whitener'.

9. Spread the lace over a clean pillow[1] and carefully pin it into shape (lace was easily pulled out of shape). If it has a 'pearl' edge (with tiny bobbles), pull these very gently into shape using the fingertips only.

10. Cover the lace with thin, clean cloth to keep dust off, and leave for two days to dry.

Removing perspiration stains and grease spots from silk, altering or refashioning last year's dresses, and invisibly mending fallen hems, split seams, rips and tears, was similarly skilled and time-consuming. So was cleaning and polishing jewellery.

Tea and sympathy

Very often, ladies' maids became their employer's close confidantes.[2] In stories – and sometimes in real life – they helped mistresses trapped in unhappy marriages or troubled by problem children, by listening to their worries, drying their tears, bringing them cups of tea, carrying secret messages – or even helping them to have love affairs or run away from

1. pillow: a lace pillow – a firm, stuffed support like a large pincushion.
2. confidante (French): a female friend who hears another woman's secrets and offers advice.

home. Victorian people were scandalised by such escapades, but still enjoyed reading about them.

'It is she [the lady's maid] who bathes Lady Theresa's eyes with eau-de-cologne after her ladyship's quarrel with the Colonel; it is she who administers sal volatile[1] to Miss Fanny when Count Beaudesert, of the Blues,[2] has deserted her... She knows by the manner in which her victim [her mistress] jerks her head from under the hairbrush, or chafes at the gentlest administration of the comb, what hidden tortures are racking her breast – what secret perplexities are bewildering her brain.'

The lady's maid also knew her mistress's beauty secrets:

'...when the ivory complexion is bought and paid for... where the pearly teeth are foreign substances fashioned by the dentist... when the glossy plaits are relics of the dead...'[3]

From Mary Elizabeth Braddon's shocking – and wildly popular – novel Lady Audley's Secret, *published in 1862*

1. *sal volatile: smelling salts – a very strong-smelling chemical used to revive women who had fainted.*
2. *a top army regiment.*
3. *long hair from very poor – or dead – women was sold to make wigs.*

Temptations

In spite of being close to her mistress in so many ways, a lady's maid was often lonely. Her mistress might be fond of her and depend on her, but she was always her superior. The maid's work required her to spend long hours alone in her lady's dressing room, and, in any case, she usually had few friends among the other servants. They envied her higher wages and easier working conditions – and also her fine clothes. A lady's maid's workwear was always smart, and rich mistresses often passed on barely worn dresses or hats, as well.

Lower servants also mocked a lady's maid's smooth speech and refined manners, which they called 'airs and graces'. If she was discreet – as her job demanded – they might accuse her of being aloof or stand-offish.

It is not surprising that ladies' maids were often tempted to 'borrow' some of their employers' finery, or at least enjoy dressing up in it – and if they were caught red-handed, they were dismissed straight away.

Back down to earth

Some loved and trusted ladies' maids stayed with the same employer all their working life. But many others found themselves without a job as they grew older. Their mistresses wanted to replace them with a younger, more energetic helper who would be more in touch with the latest designs and fashions.

And, unlike lower servants, who usually left to get married, ladies' maids – although pretty and nicely dressed – often found it difficult to acquire a husband. They never met anyone suitable, because they spent most of their time with other women: their female employer and her friends. And – unlike most lower servants – they never learned how to cook or run a home. To Victorian men in search of a wife, this was a real disadvantage.

'Cleanliness is next to Godliness,' reflected Susan

'[A] docile machine, a transferable slave –
that is their ideal of a good servant.'

Eliza Lynne Linton,
The Cornhill Magazine, 1874

HOME, SWEET HOME?

ooking needed skill and flair. Life was hectic as a lady's maid. And being a governess was grim. But Victorians knew that one of the worst jobs 'in service' was to be a maid-of-all-work: a solitary skivvy, running a whole home.

As we have seen, most Victorian families (around two-thirds of those with servants) could only afford a single 'indoor' domestic worker. This meant that half of all Victorian servants worked alone. Once or twice a week, they might have company for a few hours from a jobbing gardener, or a charwoman.

On Mondays, the laundrywoman might arrive at the crack of dawn to do the week's washing. If the maid-of-all-work was lucky – and her employers prospered – she might be joined by an errand boy or an orphan girl from the workhouse (see page 11). But more usually, she (single servants were aways female) had the responsibility for cooking, cleaning and dozens of other household tasks, all alone.

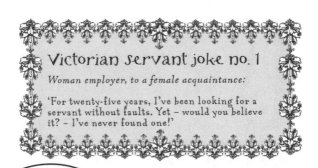

Victorian servant joke no. 1

Woman employer, to a female acquaintance:

'For twenty-five years, I've been looking for a servant without faults. Yet – would you believe it? – I've never found one!'

I can nearly see my face in it.

first steps

Why would any young woman consider such a lonely, exhausting life as a maid-of-all-work?

• First, and most importantly, because there was often no alternative. Girls from poor families needed to find a job. By the time they reached twelve or thirteen years old, their parents could no longer afford to feed or clothe them; also, many big sisters hoped to save money from their wages to train or educate their younger brothers. (In Victorian eyes, boys were more important to families than girls; they were stronger, better respected, and had greater future earning power.) As one Victorian mother said, sending her daughter off to work as a servant, 'You've got your health and strength and a good box of clothes... What in the name of goodness can a girl want with anything else?'

• Secondly, many teenage girls longed to work in a city. In their dreams, towns were places of glamour, excitement and endless possibilities – though in fact, many people who joined the Victorian 'drift to the cities' ended up struggling to survive in squalid, dangerous slums. In Victorian times, towns and cities were growing fast. The 1851 census revealed that, for the first time ever in Britain, more people were living in cities and towns than in the countryside. Fast-growing cities were full of small, lower-middle-class households striving to appear 'genteel'. To do that, they had to employ a servant – a lone maid-of-all-work – as cheaply as possible.

• Thirdly, without training, there was not much other work that young girls could do – unless they found casual, poorly paid, part-time work on farms, or were friendly with workers in factories or mines who might help them find employment. Girls brought up in sleepy country villages knew little – and probably cared less – about the dangers of life in towns. (Few Victorian parents understood the dangers of polluted city air and water, or dared to speak frankly about the city men – and women – who lured young girls into prostitution.) But, ever since they could walk and talk, country girls had been helping their mothers around the home. They were not properly trained – many had never seen new

Victorian household inventions, such as cast-iron ranges, gas lighting or flush lavatories – but they all had some experience of simple cooking and cleaning. Many had also helped care for younger brothers and sisters. In the eyes of thoughtless Victorian employers, this very basic household knowledge made them an ideal source of cheap, biddable labour.

Tricked and trapped

Some heartless employers even enticed young, inexperienced girls to work for them by offering relatively light, pleasant duties, such as being a nursemaid. The reality was often cruelly different. One girl, engaged as a nurse, was beaten by her master, who used her as a 'servant-of-all-work'. Being illiterate, she could not even let her parents know how she was being treated – until eventually a village lady wrote to them on her behalf and they came to take her home.

Not proud

There was one other, rather unexpected reason why a girl might volunteer to be a maid-of-all-work: freedom from responsibility. As a solitary maid, there was no need to co-operate with, or organise, other servants. As Victorian maid Hannah Cullwick explained in her diary in 1868:

'I dislike the thought o' being over anybody and ordering things,... for fear anyone should think me... proud.'

For freedom and true lowliness there's nothing like being a maid of all work.

The remarkable Hannah Cullwick (see page 51): a maid-of-all-work and proud of it

Round the clock

So! Imagine that you're an innocent young teenager, newly arrived in a big city. You've got a job as a maid-of-all-work. What will your duties be? Of course, the precise details of your work will vary from household to household. All employers have their own pet likes and dislikes, and their own (sometimes very!) peculiar habits. But – if you can read – we suggest you consult Mrs Beeton as your guide. She sets out a handy timetable to take you through a typical day's work. But be warned! It's exhausting – and you'll need an awful lot of aprons!

We've based this chart on Mrs Beeton's book:

5.00 a.m. Get up.

5.30 a.m. Open downstairs shutters and windows.

6.00 a.m. Brush kitchen range, light its firebox, clean its hearth, polish all its shiny bits 'as rapidly and vigorously as possible'.

6.30 a.m. Put on big kettle of water to boil. Clean dining room: roll up rug, lift fender, shake and fold tablecloth, sweep the floor, clean the fireplace, clear away ashes, replace fender, light fire, dust the whole room (ash from the fire will have blown everywhere), replace rug, replace tablecloth. Lay table for breakfast, shut dining-room door (because it must appear as if you have never been in it – the room is a private space for your employers).

7.30 a.m. Sweep the hall, shake the mats, clean the doorstep, polish the door handles. Clean whole family's boots, including children's.

8.00 a.m. Wash your hands and face (which will by now be dusty and dirty), and put on a clean white apron, ready to serve breakfast.

8.30 a.m. Fill heavy urn with boiling water from kettle and carry it to the dining room so that your employer can make tea or coffee when she's ready. Cook bacon, kidneys, fish etc. for family breakfast; lay out plates of cold meat; bring bread, rolls, butter, preserves to dining room; make hot toast.

If there's time, grab a quick breakfast – just bread and butter, probably. Your employer might give you tea and sugar to make your own drinks as part of your wages.

9.00 a.m. While the family are still having breakfast, go upstairs to the bedrooms, open the windows, take the sheets and blankets off the beds so that the air may freshen them.

9.30 a.m. Go downstairs again. Clear the breakfast plates etc. from the dining room; sweep the floor and the hearth; leave the room clean and tidy.

10.00 a.m. Go to the kitchen; wash up breakfast dishes. Clean and tidy the kitchen. Listen – as politely as you can – while your employer gives you orders for the day.

Scrub scrub

Achooo!

10.30 a.m. Go to the bedrooms again, carrying slop pail, jug of hot water, and cloths. Empty the chamberpots into the slop pail, rinse them with hot water, and dry them. Make the beds. NB: Put on a big, wide apron first, so that the dirt from your working clothes does not soil the clean bedlinen! If they're not too grand, perhaps your employer or her daughter will help you.

How to make beds – Victorian style

You don't just shake the duvet! Victorians slept in beds made of feathers, covered with linen sheets and woollen blankets. The feather bed stood on a wooden or metal bed frame, which was topped by a thick palliasse – a padded mat, usually stuffed with horsehair or straw – and an under-mattress.

- Pull back bedcovers.

- Open bedroom window.

- Leave the bed to air for at least an hour.

- Turn the under-mattress and palliasse once a week, then:

'every morning,... shake all the feathers from each corner of the bed then turn it half over, and knead and pinch the feathers with both hands, then turn it quite over, then shake it at each corner again before... [pushing]...the feathers into shape. And... take care to have rather more feathers at the top end than the bottom...'

'Mrs Motherly', The Servants' Behaviour Book, 1859

Watch out for these!

Bedbug

11.00 a.m. Dust the bedrooms and the stairs. Sweep the drawing-room floor. Your employer might prefer to dust the drawing room herself. As Mrs Beeton says: 'A maid-of-all-work's hands are not always in a condition to handle delicate ornaments.' (Can you think why this might be?)

Victorian servant joke no. 2

Maid-of-all-work, telling a friend about her new job:

'I've agreed to pay for all I break, but I don't mind, as I never break nothing – it's always the cat!'

Skid!

11.30 a.m. Change from bed-making apron into a thick, coarse one – it's better for doing dirty work in. Start to prepare dinner. Maybe your employer will help with the cooking. With luck, she'll teach you some of her recipes.

12.30 p.m. Go to dining room. Lay the table for dinner – or luncheon. (Different families eat their main meal at different times of the day; an evening dinner is newfangled, and more fashionable.) Put bread, salt, water etc. on the table, ready and waiting.

1.00 p.m. Dinner is served! In fact, you serve it. Hand round the main course, then hurry back to the kitchen to make sure that the pudding course is ready. After a suitable pause, carry that to the dining room and serve it, too.

1.30 p.m. Clear the dining table, sweep the floor and hearth, dust the furniture. Clean and light the parlour fire, if you have not already lit it this morning. NB: All through the day, you'll have to keep the home fires burning – and carry coal upstairs to wherever it is needed. A servant can lose her job for letting the fires go out!

2.00 p.m. Now, for the first time today (according to Mrs Beeton), you can sit down – and eat your own dinner. You'll probably have what's left over from the family's meal.

2.30 p.m. Wash up the dinner plates etc., dry them and put them away. Sweep, dust and tidy the kitchen (yet again!). If there are any more boots and shoes to clean, do that now, together with any other dirty work, such as cleaning knives.

3.30 p.m. Get changed into your other, cleaner dress (you probably only have two). Just possibly, you might be able to sit down again for an hour or so right now – but don't be idle! There will always be sewing or mending for the household to be getting on with.

5.00 p.m. Make and serve tea (and little sandwiches, and cake) to your employer and her guests.

6.00 p.m. Take tea cups and plates etc. from dining room or parlour. Wash them up and put them away. Tidy kitchen.

6.30 p.m. Go upstairs to bedrooms. Fill bedside water bottles and jugs. Close the windows; draw the curtains or blinds.

7.00 p.m. Make and serve supper.

8.00 p.m. Wash supper plates etc. and put them away. Find kindling to light the kitchen range and other fires tomorrow, and stack it neatly close by the range to dry (that way, it will light more easily).

8.30 p.m. Perhaps you can sit down again for an hour or so, by yourself, in the kitchen. It's not wise to go to bed until you're sure that your employer will have no other orders for you. Take this chance to do a little more needlework, or read an 'improving' book, ideally with a religious theme.

So lonely

'They think that the cat and the kettle, and the kitchen clock, are company enough for a poor servant. They never think of us in the long winter nights, when they are playing at cards, or chatting with folks who've dropt in – they never think of us, all alone as we are, without a soul to speak to! No; we must have no followers,[1] though, perhaps, the parlour's[2] ringing again with laughter; and our only chance of opening our lips is the chance of being sent out to get oysters[3] for the company.'

Punch, 1844

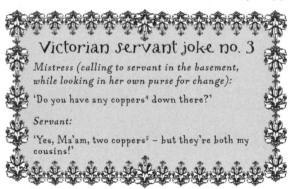

Victorian servant joke no. 3

Mistress (calling to servant in the basement, while looking in her own purse for change):

'Do you have any coppers[4] down there?'

Servant:

'Yes, Ma'am, two coppers[5] – but they're both my cousins!'

1. *boyfriends.*
2. *elegant sitting room, where employers welcomed their friends.*
3. *favourite takeaway supper; had to be purchased and eaten very fresh.*
4. *small coins.*
5. *junior policemen.*

Don't *let* them in!

Yes, you'll be lonely, but don't let that dashing young soldier who saluted you on the doorstep, or the butcher's cheery errand boy, or the gossipy groom from over the road come to keep you company. Your mistress will scold you for entertaining 'followers' – and may even dismiss you.

Oh, Albert, we mustn't be seen like this!

10.30 p.m. Bedtime (at last)! Lock and bolt all the doors, then stagger – very, very sleepily – upstairs to bed. Say your prayers, and drift off to sleep thinking wistfully of your family and home in the country. How is your mother? Your father? Your big brother Joe and your little sister Lizzie? How's your best friend Sue? She went to work in a stately home as a scullery maid. And how's Jim the ploughboy, who's *so* good-looking? You sigh as you remember that it will be almost a year before you see any of them again – you don't get much holiday.

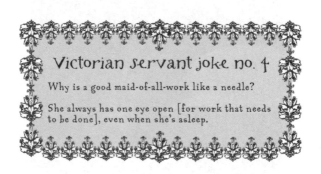

Victorian servant joke no. 4

Why is a good maid-of-all-work like a needle?

She always has one eye open [for work that needs to be done], even when she's asleep.

2.00 a.m. HORRORS! You wake up in a panic. What day will it be tomorrow? Or is it tomorrow already? According to Mrs Beeton, each day has extra household tasks for you, as well as your regular duties.

Weekly tasks

Can you remember what you have to do tomorrow? Let Mrs Beeton remind you:

Monday: Clean the drawing room or parlour; this includes washing the windows and polishing all the furniture.

Tuesday: Clean two of the bedrooms.

Wednesday: Clean two more bedrooms – and remember to sweep under the bed this time!

Thursday: Clean any more bedrooms, and the stairs. Those twiddly carved wooden banisters are very difficult to polish!

Friday: Clean the dining room and hall. Oh, and polish all the saucepans and cooking pots.

Saturday: Polish all the silver dishes and cutlery. Clean the kitchen, 'arranging everything in nice order'.

'The maid of all work, if she wish to retain her situation,[1] must be industrious, cleanly, and thoughtful, and not only able to work, but to plan.'

From The Dictionary of Daily Wants, *1858–1859*

1. keep her job.

fact and fiction

The most famous portrayal of a happy Victorian maid-of-all-work appeared in Mrs Gaskell's novel Cranford, *first published in book form in 1853.*

Martha, a 'rough, honest-looking country girl', has come to work for Miss Matilda ('Matty'), a very kindly, thoughtful old lady. Miss Matty has never married, but was once, long ago, in love. She has just received news that her former sweetheart has died:

The evening of the day on which we heard of Mr Holbrook's death, Miss Matilda was very silent and thoughtful; after prayers she called Martha back and then she stood uncertain what to say.

'Martha!' she said, at last, 'you are young' – and then she made so long a pause that Martha, to remind her of her half-finished sentence, dropped a curtsey, and said –

'Yes, please, ma'am; two-and-twenty last third of October, please, ma'am.'

'And, perhaps, Martha, you may some time meet with a young man you like, and who likes you. I did say you were not to have followers; but if you meet with such a young man, and tell me, and I find he is respectable, I have no objection to his coming to see you once a week. God forbid!' said she in a low voice, 'that I should grieve any young hearts.' She spoke as if she were providing for some distant contingency,[1] and was rather startled when Martha made her ready eager answer –

'Please, ma'am, there's Jem Hearn, and he's a joiner making three-and-sixpence a-day, and six foot one in his stocking-feet, please, ma'am; and if you'll ask about him to-morrow morning, every one will give him a character for steadiness; and he'll be glad enough to come to-morrow night, I'll be bound.'

Though Miss Matty was startled, she submitted to Fate and Love.

Cranford *is a novel, but here is a real-life example of kindness to a servant. 'Poor Peggy' was out of work and had had a troubled life:*

My Father having told her story to Alderman Atkins, she [Peggy] was taken into that good man's family to attend his invalid wife, a service she faithfully performed... She died of consumption some years after this, most carefully nursed, poor thing, by those kind people who had become quite attached to her.

Elizabeth Grant, Memoirs of a Highland Lady *(written 1840s, published 1898)*

1. *some event in the far future.*

Seeking and hoping

It is hardly surprising that few maids-of-all-work stayed in the same household for many years. Instead, they moved from job to job, hoping to find better wages or 'easier' employers. Such people did exist – the Victorians themselves said that 'a limited [small] family of regular habits' would be the best kind of household to work in, and recognised that at least some employers might have 'a disposition to treat the servant [i.e. maid] with kindness and consideration'.

> Mistress and I get on well enough now I've got used to her little ways.

A home of her own!

Even better than hunting for a kind employer, a teenage (or twenty-something) maid-of-all-work longed to find a husband. Marriage brought (she hoped) love, companionship – and children – and literally 'opened the door' to a new, independent lifestyle. Her new home would probably be very poor, and her workload just as exhausting. But, as a married woman, she would be respected much more than she had been as a servant – and she would be free!

Bless him! He's less trouble than my old master.

A governess did not always enjoy the respect she deserved

'Society has thought fit to assert that a woman who works for herself loses her social position.'

Elizabeth M. Sewell, Principles of Education, *1865*

CHAPTER SIX

'SEDENTARY, SOLITARY, CONSTRAINED, JOYLESS, TOILSOME'[1]

A 'lady' *and* a servant! The Victorian governess was in an impossible position. Her family and friends pitied her; her employers looked down on her, however kindly they treated her. Other servants disliked and distrusted her. She was not 'one of them': her clothes, speech, manners, family background and (probably) tastes and interests were different from theirs, and they suspected her of snobbishness. The children she cared for, sensing her awkward position, often teased or disobeyed her.

1. *The life of a governess, described by novelist Charlotte Brontë in* Shirley, *1849.*

And how did the governess herself feel? As well as being exasperated or angry with naughty children, she was almost certainly sad, anxious and very, very lonely. In any household, from one to a hundred servants, she had no close comrade and no equal. For all these reasons, few Victorian women ever *chose* to become a governess. ('Anything but that!' exclaimed one horrified mother.)

Lost and gone

For anyone brought up as a Victorian 'lady', having to work – even in genteel surroundings in a fine country house – was a sign of terrible failure. It signalled loss: loss of home and family, money and privilege, lifestyle and personal identity, social contacts and status. It meant leaving the 'best circles' for a very uncertain future. Too old to go on teaching, many elderly governesses ended their lives in the workhouse, alongside beggars, homeless people and out-of-work labourers.

If life as a governess was so very miserable, why did so many women – young and not so young – try to become one? Census returns reveal that there were at least 21,000 working governesses in 1851. Newspapers carried advertisements every day, placed by women seeking 'situations':

'AS COMPANION or Nursery Governess – A young lady, age 20, wishes to obtain a SITUATION…. She is acquainted with the rudiments of an English education, and is a good needlewoman. No objection to travel…'

Advertisement in The Times, *1853*

As well as newspaper advertisements, there were also employment agencies (often fraudulent) offering to find jobs for would-be governesses, and quack 'consultants', like the man who charged a fee to examine applicants' skulls to check whether they would be suitable.[1] From 1843, the highly respectable Governesses' Benevolent Institution provided a safer, more trustworthy employment service, as well as help for governesses who could not work because they were old or ill. In 1848, Queen's College in London was set up to train governesses – and to try to win respect for their professional skills. Still, most women became governesses for one simple reason: they had no other way of providing themselves with a home, food and clothing.

1. Assessing a person's character by feeling the shape of their head was called 'phrenology'; many people regarded it as a real science.

Doomed to be a governess?

Tick more than a few of these boxes – and a governess you must be!

☐ Are you a lady? Do you have 'breeding' (upper-class upbringing and family connections)?

☐ Are you refined? Do you know all the rules of polite society?

☐ Are you well-spoken, with a 'nice' accent?

☐ Are you educated? Do you read and write English and French? Have you studied history, geography, poetry? Do you know German or Italian?

☐ Do you have 'accomplishments'? Can you paint, sing, dance, play the piano, embroider?

☐ Is your father a 'gentleman'? Perhaps a merchant, surgeon, army or navy officer, government official, lawyer or clergyman?

☐ Has he lost money, fallen ill, or had bad luck?

☐ Has your father died and your mother remarried? Is your stepfather unwilling to support you?

☐ Are you an orphan, without rich relations who are willing to care for you?

I don't seem to have much choice, then!

☐ Have you got lots of sisters? If your family can't afford to arrange 'suitable' marriages for them all, it's better not to wed than to marry 'beneath your station'. That would make your whole family lose respect and status.

☐ Do you have younger brothers to help or support?

☐ Are you an old maid or a widow, with no man to support you?

☐ Are you homeless, or about to lose your home?

☐ Do you come from a middle-class family, but hope to rise in society?

☐ Can you think of any alternative profession that's open to respectable women? (No, in early Victorian times – before about 1870 – there really isn't one. Writing's uncertain; needlecraft doesn't pay enough; nursing and teaching are still deeply unrespectable.)

Above all, a governess must be *moral*. That's what really matters. As a 19th-century writer explained:

> 'Many mothers…will gladly engage a governess who will do the great work of education – and will employ masters for the less important one of teaching.'

Mary Atkinson Maurice, Governess Life, Its Trials and Duties, *1849*

Of course, you'll be religious, but you mustn't hold extreme or unusual beliefs. That would upset your employers – you might 'infect' the children with your 'outrageous' ideas.

Mama says you had to be a governess because your papa lost all his money.

Anything else?

Still can't face the prospect of becoming a governess and living like a second-class servant among people of equal rank to your own?

• You could try taking a few 'respectable' children into your home, and teaching them there. But that's risky.

• You could visit rich people's homes (like a tradesman!) to give daily lessons to their children. But that's degrading – and exhausting. You'd spend hours on the public (ugh! shudder!) omnibus!

• If you are lucky enough to live at the end of Queen Victoria's reign, then – Heaven be praised! – you will find a wider choice of careers for educated, respectable women. You might work in an office, train to be a doctor, nurse or teacher, study at college, open a shop, or operate that marvel of new technology – the telephone!

Meanwhile...

Back in mid-Victorian times, you can't yet make those career choices. So you accept your fate: you'll be a governess. What will your duties be? Another mixture – this time, of mothering and teaching. This uneasy mix makes it difficult to pass on your knowledge and accomplishments in a detached and professional way. It also means that the children's real mother will feel entitled – or even obliged – to interfere. After all, your pupils are her offspring, and Victorians believe that there is a sacred, special bond of trust between a mother and her children. Even Queen Victoria herself interrupted her children's lessons.

Another problem: you'll be expected to show devotion to your pupils, just like any mother; but you must not encourage them to care for you in return – they must save all their love for their mother. Be very careful! You're all alone – and lonely. Children are (mostly) lovable. Don't get too fond of them. One day, you'll have to leave. That would break your heart.

A governess's day

You'll have a lot of time to fill! Nursery routine is strict – and ruled by the head nurse (by late Victorian times, called 'Nanny'). She will make sure that the nursemaids and junior nursemaids keep your pupils washed, cleanly dressed and well fed. She may sometimes ask you to help with these duties, though strictly speaking they are not your responsibility.

Victorians believe that children learn best early in the morning; 7.00 a.m. is therefore a good time to start lessons. Here's how one girl and her governess spent a typical day around 1890:

7.00 a.m. Get up
Piano practice

8.00 a.m. Breakfast
Practise writing in copybook
Maths
History

11.00 a.m. Break time!
Geography
Poetry

1.00 p.m. Lunch
Well-earned rest!

2.00 p.m. Bible study
Story time

3.00 p.m. Fresh air at last! – a long walk

5.00 p.m. Teatime

6.00 p.m. Sewing

6.30 p.m. Reading a story aloud

7.00 p.m. Bathtime and bed.

Essential equipment

As well as access to the family piano (and, if possible, harp), a governess's pupils should also have:

- copybooks (for practising neat handwriting) and books about maths

- books of general knowledge and 'elegant literature', such as poetry

- a Bible and books of Christian stories

- books on geography, and a pair of globes

- books on popular science, a microscope and a telescope

- and – guess what? – a guitar!

Joining in?

Once the children are in bed, you must change into a neat, demure frock and prepare to join your employers as they chat in the drawing room after dinner. But you won't be welcome if they have guests to dinner. You would be an embarrassment. The gentlemen can't be gallant, because you're a servant – and they'll never think of befriending you, because that would 'lower' them. The ladies can't share their secrets, because you work for pay. So – go back to your lonely room! Stay away!

You must always, always, always keep strict control of your behaviour:

> 'The governess who desires to be on a footing with the family, ought to be able to conduct herself in such manner, as never to render an apology necessary for her presence at family parties.'

S. and S. Adams, The Complete Servant, 1825

In other words, censor your own thoughts, words, deeds – and feelings – and try to be invisible. In so many ways, alas, you might as well not exist!

A vision of the good life

'As the coach rolls swiftly past the fields and orchards,... women and children... pause for an instant from their labour, and... gaze upon the passengers with curious eyes, while some stout urchin, too small to work,... scrambles over the side of the basket in which he has been deposited for security, and kicks and screams with delight...'

Charles Dickens, The Pickwick Papers, *1836–1837*

CHAPTER SEVEN

DOWN ON THE FARM

In 1837, the first year of Queen Victoria's reign, novelist Charles Dickens described in *The Pickwick Papers* an idyllic summer scene, full of smiling, suntanned farm workers. Dickens was contrasting a smart, flashy, untrustworthy town-based coach – and its occupants – with slower, gentler country ways.

But novels are not real life. What looked charming and romantic to Dickens was, in fact, dirty, monotonous and exhausting – especially in cold, wet wintertime.

Around 1870, for example, ten-year-old Tom Mullins went to work on a farm in the north of England. He was given food and lodgings, and a wage of £3 a year – that's enough to buy about two loaves of bread every three days. He was always hungry, and often had no dry clothes to wear. On Sundays he walked home to his parents' house for dinner – a journey of 10 miles (16 km) each way.

food and farming

At the beginning of Queen Victoria's reign, more people in Britain worked on farms than in any other occupation. Unlike today, when much food eaten in the UK is imported, Victorian farm workers – women as well as men – fed the nation by ploughing fields to plant potatoes, wheat (for bread) and barley (for beer), raising cows for milk and cheese, rearing pigs, sheep and cattle to be slaughtered for meat, and keeping chickens to lay eggs. Thousands more country men and women grew – and laboriously picked by hand – fresh fruit and vegetables to be sold in towns. Farm workers also bred horses to provide transport.

Sad to say, many could not afford to eat the foods they produced. For six days a week they ate bread or potatoes, fatty bacon and vegetables. They had fresh meat (usually pork) only as a treat on Sundays.

Cosy cottages?

Most farm workers were labourers; that is, they were hired by the day, month or year to work when they were needed, for example at harvest time. Labourers lived in their own homes, which were usually rented cottages. If they were lucky, worked hard, found well-paid jobs and saved every penny, they might also rent a couple of fields and keep a cow or some sheep, to earn extra money. Or they might buy extra food, or firewood to keep warm in winter. But if they became too old or ill to work, they had to rely on charity, or their children. And guess what most of those were doing (especially the daughters)? Yes, of course, they were working as domestic servants.

Home on the farm

Farm servants, unlike day labourers, had no homes of their own. They lived on the farms where they worked: they slept indoors (often on the floor in the kitchen) if they helped the farmer's wife with household chores or childcare; outdoors in dormitory blocks, or above stables, or in rough huts (called *bothies*, especially in Scotland), if they worked in the fields or cared for livestock. Food was plentiful, but extremely boring:

'...jist as it grew on the farm. Ye got yer brose in the morning...then ye had neeps, neep-brose, kale and kale-brose, sowans...'[1]

A Scottish farm servant – who added that servants occasionally stole a chicken, but then had to find a way of cooking it secretly and disposing of the feathers!

Worth every penny!

Like household servants, farm labourers and farm servants were recruited through word of mouth, newspaper advertisements or hiring

1. *brose: oatmeal broth; neeps: swedes (a root vegetable); kale: cabbage; sowans: oat-bran porridge.*

fairs (also called 'mop fairs'; see page 135). Wages for skilled work, such as ploughing or running a dairy, were higher than those paid to most household servants, but all farmwork, whoever did it, was probably more exhausting than domestic chores, and often distinctly unpleasant. To fertilise the fields, for example, cows' urine was collected in tanks and carted out to the fields in barrels. Then it was poured onto the ground using a special long-handled ladle. Women walked after the horses that grazed in the pastures, breaking up the dung they dropped behind them using a long fork.

Bottom of the heap

Some farm servants were young men and girls at the start of their careers; others had special skills such as making cheese, or caring for carthorses. But many were widows, orphaned teenagers, older unmarried people, or mothers whose menfolk had deserted them. They found shelter on farms and worked there when they were needed; some also took on piecework,[1] such as sewing. It was a struggle for them to survive.

1. *work done for a fixed payment for each item completed.*

from the 1891 census, Perthshire, Scotland

Building	Occupants	Age	Employment
Little Powgavie Farm Cottar House[1]	Helen Kerr	40	Outworker[2]
	Annie McDonnell[3]	30	Nurse[maid]
	David R. Johnston	13	Outworker
	Helena McDonnell	2	
	John McDonnell	2	
	Donald K. McDonnell	10 months	
Little Powgavie Farm	John D. Anton	21	Farm Servant
Bothy	Thomas Elder	21	Farm Servant

1. See next page.
2. This probably means an odd-job farm worker.
3. The author's great-grandmother. Helen Kerr was Annie's aunt.

Ideal home vs. rough reality

'No cottage ought to be erected which does not contain a warm, comfortable, plain room, with an oven to bake the bread of its occupier; a small closet for the beer and provisions, two wholesome lodging rooms, one whereof should be for the man and his wife, and the other for his children.'

O. Gwilt, An Encyclopaedia of Architecture, 1876

'Cot-houses [or Cottars' houses]... were usually irregular structures attached to the end of farm houses or offices [farm buildings] and "were generally inhabited by people of extreme indigence [poverty]." They measured about 12 or 13 square feet [i.e. feet square],[1] had a damp floor and lacked partitions, inner doors, smoke-funnels, glass in the window, and decent furniture...

'On one estate in south-west Scotland, "some people lived in disused dog-kennels converted for their use."

'In other cottages, the rain was "kept out by guano[2] bags stretched across the rafters".'

Jean Aitchison, Servants in Ayrshire 1750–1914, 2001

1. 3.6–4 metres square.
2. guano: dried, solidified bird droppings, collected and used as crop fertiliser. The bags were made of sacking.

No time to rest?

Farm servants' housing was grim. Even worse, hard-working servants often had little time to rest in it. In 1894, UK government inspectors were horrified to discover that dairymaids were expected to start work at 4.00 a.m., ploughmen at 5.00 a.m. and fieldworkers at 7.00 a.m., or first light in winter. Most farm servants were allowed a long break at lunchtime, but then had to work again until 7.00 or 8.00 p.m., although fieldworkers could stop in winter as soon as darkness fell.

Somehow, farm servants still found the energy to enjoy themselves, by singing, dancing – and making up rude songs about the farmers who employed them. In this bothy ballad,[1] the singer comes from a sailor's family, but has been working as a ploughman:

1. *bothy ballad: a song sung by farm servants for their own entertainment in the bothy at the end of the working day.*

The Scranky Farmer

At the tap o' the Garioch, in the lands of
    Leith-Hall,[1]
A scranky black farmer in Earlsfield did dwell;
Wi' him I engaged a servant to be,
Which makes me lament I went far from the sea.

I engaged wi' this farmer to drive cart and ploo;
Haed fortune convenit an ill-fated crew,
I ane of the number, which causes me rue
That e'er I attempted the country to view.

It's early in the mornin' we rise to the yoke,
The storm and the tempest can ne'er make
    us stop;
While the wind it does beat, and the rain it
    does pour,
And aye yon black farmer on us does glowre.

Bothy

1. All the places mentioned are in Aberdeenshire, north-east Scotland.

[tap: top; scranky: mean, scrawny; black: dark-haired; engaged wi':
made a bargain with; ploo: plough; haed: here had; convenit: called
together; I ane: I was one; rue: regret; aye: always; glowre: glower, look
mean and angry.]

On the move

Unlike farm labourers, who often stayed in the same cottages for generations, homeless farm servants travelled long distances, desperate to find work and shelter. Where did they go?

- from the countryside to the cities, to work in factories, railways, foundries – and as household servants.

- from the bleak upland areas of Britain to gentler, more prosperous and productive lowland farms.

- from poor villages throughout the UK to join the army; Queen Victoria's troops were fighting in many lands, especially in Africa and India.

- overseas, to America, Canada, Australia, New Zealand. Over two million men, women and children left Ireland and Scotland after the disastrous potato famines of the 1840s, and after Scottish landlords changed from raising cattle and growing grain to intensive sheep farming, dramatically reducing the need for farmworkers of all kinds.

Cut and run

- Fed up with farmers?
- Envious of employers?
- Could you consider cheating?
- Don't mind leaving the district?

Then be a slippery servant – wreak your revenge this way!

Go to a hiring fair, strike a deal with a farmer to work with him for six months, take his shilling (a silver coin – the sign that a deal has been done) – and then disappear! Many, many farm servants have done this. It's easy money, so long as you don't ever show your face in the neighbourhood again.

Hundreds of farmworkers and their families were drowned in shipwrecks before they could start a new life in a new land. Others disappeared soon after going ashore: no-one knows what happened to them. But many overseas Britons prospered and became farmers themselves. Some even employed native peoples as servants – but that is another story.

Stepney, Oct. 9th

MADAM,

Having heard you are in want of a housemaid, I venture to apply for the situation. I have been four years in my last place, and can produce a good character[1] for honesty, order, and industry; and I may venture to say that I think I should suit you, having been accustomed to service from a little child. My wages are twelve pounds a year. Should you feel disposed to give me a trial, you would much oblige,

Your humble servant,
MARY ANN MARSH.

Maida Hill, Oct. 10th.

Mary Ann Marsh,

Bring your character to-morrow. I think very likely you would suit me. Early rising and personal neatness are two things which I expect of those in my service; and if you are not in the habit of practising both, it is needless for you to come.

Emily Mordaunt.

Two sample letters (note the difference in tone!) from a Victorian book of advice, The Ladies' and Gentlemen's Model Letter Writer, c.1870

1. character: written reference from previous employer(s).

CHAPTER EIGHT

A GOOD CHARACTER

In 1879, *The Times* newspaper in London printed a letter from one of its readers. The writer made a suggestion that seems quite outrageous today. (To be fair, many Victorians did not like it, either.) He proposed that each servant should be issued – by the police, no less – with a blank book containing numbered pages. Starting on page 1, each new employer should write a 'character' (reference) for the servant, adding extra remarks about their work, appearance, habits, morals and so on, as they thought fit.

Servants would be ordered not to remove any pages from the book, no matter what unkind, unjust or unflattering comments had been written about them. But if they did so, the numbers on the pages would show that some were missing. This would arouse suspicion in any employer's mind, and make it very difficult for the servant, now labelled as 'a bad character', to get another job.

A real 'lady'?

What had servants done to make people want to treat them with such distrust, as if they were criminals? Nothing in particular. The writer was just voicing, in an extreme way, the anxiety felt by the new servant-keeping middle class of Victorian Britain.

As early as the 1840s, people were making jokes about this:

'[The best way to make an employer agree with the way you want to work is] by declaring that you never heard of any "lady" requiring whatever it may be that you have set your face against. By laying stress on the word "lady", you show your knowledge of the habits of the superior classes; and as the person hiring you will probably wish to imitate their ways, she will perhaps take your hint as to what a "lady" ought to do.'

Punch (a humorous magazine), 1845

The writer is mocking sly, scheming servants, as well as snobbish middle-class employers.

Band of brothers... and sisters

Later, by the 1870s, so many people wanted domestic help that servants began to make organised public demands for better treatment. These were supported by Victorian social reformers, and inspired by workers in factories and mines, who joined together in trades unions. The first servants' unions were set up in 1872, in Dundee and Leamington. But the servants came from such downtrodden families, lived such isolated lives, and were so seldom free to attend meetings, that the unions did not survive. Servants had to wait until the 20th century before they won any real workers' rights.

Strange but true no. 1

The Dundee maids protested because they were forced to wear a rather silly headdress as a sign of their servant status. Nicknamed 'the flag', it was tall and flapped above their heads as they worked. How irritating!

The maids also demanded – but did not get – half a day free from work each week, a whole day off on alternate Sundays, and payment every three months rather than half-yearly.

Into service

So, being a Victorian servant meant submitting yourself to a powerful employer for all your working life – but, as we saw in Chapter 1, for many Victorians there was not much alternative. Picture yourself as a country boy or girl near the start of Queen Victoria's reign (1837):

It's here! The day you've been dreading and, just maybe, also looking forward to. It's time for you to leave home! Your parents can no longer afford to feed you, and their tiny, crowded cottage has no room for you any more. So, take a deep breath, put on a brave smile, and wave goodbye to your childhood! You're only 12 years old, but it's time to join the grown-up world of work and worry.

Where can you find a job that will feed and clothe you and provide a roof over your head – and let you save enough to send money back home to your family? Well, with very little education and no special skills, you don't have many choices. You follow your parents' advice and decide to be a servant.

Seek and find

Like most other country children, you've never left your village. How will you find a job, and where will you go?

Job-hunting is a problem. There are no phones, no Internet and, even if you can read, you can't afford to buy a newspaper. That's how some rich families advertise their needs, and well-etablished servants announce that they are looking for 'situations'.

Put your thinking cap on! There must be something you can do!

- Ask your family, friends and neighbours. That's how most servants find employment. Isn't your auntie's best friend's sister a housemaid somewhere?

- Beg your mother or father to get dressed in their best (their only?) decent clothes, remember their most respectful manners, and call on the butler or housekeeper of the nearest stately home.

- Go and see the vicar, or, more likely, his wife. Yes, she's a bossy busybody, but she has a kind heart and likes to help the poor. A recommendation from her should mean a good start to your career.

- Talk to local shopkeepers. They hear all the local gossip, and see servants or mistresses every day as customers.

- Apply to an agency. Many new ones will be opening throughout Queen Victoria's reign. But beware! Some are not what they seem. They kidnap young girls, and sell them to be sex workers. Others promise to find you a job, take your money – and then do nothing.

- Go to an old-fashioned 'mop fair'. Held once a year, these are a cross between a cattle market and a jolly day out. Servants stand holding the tools of their trade (housemaids carry mops or brooms), while employers walk around inspecting them and, perhaps, choosing one.

- Ask a charity. If you're an orphan, or from the workhouse, this will be almost your only chance of finding a job as a servant. In fact, you'll be forced to take one – or starve on the streets! Later in the century, organisations like the Girls Friendly Society (set up by the Church of England in 1875) might be able to help you.

I think we have just the right situation for you, my dear.

Do you tick the right boxes?

Are you:	Yes	No
1. Healthy?	☐	☐
2. Strong?	☐	☐
3. Willing?	☐	☐
4. Ready to learn?	☐	☐
5. Trained?	☐	☐
6. Uniformed?	☐	☐
7. Married?	☐	☐
8. With a good 'character'?	☐	☐

Correct answers:

1, 2, 3, 4: Yes.

5 and 6: Yes, but only if you're already a servant. Otherwise you'll be trained as you work, and you'll have to save up money to make or buy your own working clothes.

7: No. Most employers will dismiss you if you marry.

8: Yes. You'll have to ask for a written reference each time you leave an employer.

A GOOD CHARACTER

So you've passed the test and been offered your first job. Pack your shabby carpet bag or your little tin trunk. Kiss your family goodbye, and off you go!

'I had an extra pair of trousers, a change of underclothes and five apples. With fivepence in my pockets, I walked five miles to begin my career.'

Footboy in a grand country house, 1870

'As Mama walked away, I realised that I was alone for the first time in my life.'

Pageboy, 1894

Hi-ho!

Strange but true no. 2

So many young girls left home to work as servants in Victorian times, that country villages soon ran short of women. There was no-one for young men to marry!

Away from home - alone

It is no surprise to learn that many new servants soon felt 'homesick and heartsick'. They would not see their family for a year, and their new homes were horrible:

'She comes up from the country and is plunged at once from the fresh air and free expanse of her old surroundings into the dismal darkness of a London kitchen.'

Social reformer Eliza Lynne Linton in
The Cornhill Magazine, *1874*

Employers preferred servants who came from at least 20 miles away; it discouraged servants' friends from visiting, and stopped miserable young maids from running back home. In any case, servants did not have the money, the free time, or their employer's permission to travel:

'The kindest-hearted mistress treats it as an impertinence when her maid stipulates [asks] for rights, say in the matter of a fixed holiday.'

Eliza Lynne Linton, 1874

Some servants were well fed and housed, but many found themselves cold and hungry.

Even in grand houses, servants' rooms were often dark and miserable, and their food was prepared by inexperienced kitchen maids. In small households, conditions might be worse:

'I really believe servants only feel happy if their rooms... resemble the homes of their youth... merely places where they lie down to sleep as heavily as they can. The simpler, therefore, a servant's room is furnished, the better.'

Victorian advice-writer Mrs Panton, 1880

'The cook and the housekeeper had nice beds, but we had only chaff[1] sacks. We brought our own blankets, so, as we were four to a bed we were not cold.'

...

'I have seen many a more comfortable hen-house.'

Servant and fisherwoman Christian Watt (1833–1923), describing servants' bothies (sleeping huts) in northern Scotland

1. *husks of grain.*

Strange but true no. 3

Victorian country girls had often never seen a cast-iron cooking range before, and did not know how to light it or cook on it. They also had to be taught the names of fancy household furnishings and kitchen utensils. Only rich homes had those!

Onwards and upwards

A young servant who survived the first few years in service might begin to look for a job with more generous pay and greater freedom. Many servants changed jobs every three or four years. Where might you look for a more interesting situation?

- Enjoy crowds, bright lights, glamour, excitement? Choose a bustling seaside resort like Brighton or Blackpool.

- Long to be surrounded by culture, history, politics and power? Then head for London, Britain's capital city.

- Hope to see High Society? Then find work in refined and elegant cities such as Bath, where posh people live.

- **Want to see the world?** Find an Army or Navy family to work for. They're often posted overseas to run the British Empire.

- **Desperate but demanding?** Head to the north of England. Servants are very scarce there (boys and girls go to work in factories, instead), so you should get a good deal from your employer!

A trained, experienced servant had useful skills to sell, and, with luck, a good character reference. By the end of Victoria's reign, this made them more confident and more choosy. One girl even suggested that servants interview mistresses. Were they good-tempered, generous with food, kindly, encouraging, not always suspicious, scolding, nagging?

As she explained:

'You see,... it is as necessary that girls should have characters with[1] the mistresses, as that mistresses should have characters with the girls.'

Letter from a maidservant to a newspaper, 1888

1. *obtain references for.*

Susan is a credit to her employers

'A gaudily dressed servant looks, at best, like a coarse and vulgar lady... but a neatly dressed girl... does not draw attention to the natural distinctions between a hard-working woman and a lady.'

'Mrs Motherly', The Servants' Behaviour Book, 1859

CHAPTER NINE

THEM AND US

Victorians liked to think of themselves as upright, God-fearing, honest, honourable, deeply moral people. They said their prayers, read their Bibles, gave money to charity, visited the poor, set up committees to do 'good works', and joined countless campaigns to improve society in all ways imaginable, from abolishing slavery to opening ladies' public lavatories.[1]

1. Slavery was abolished in Britain in 1833. Female public lavatories, first opened in London in 1851, made it possible for 'respectable' women to stay away from home for more than a few hours at a time. This freed them to take part in all kinds of public activities, from studying in libraries or visiting museums to lobbying Parliament. The campaign for more women's lavatories was spearheaded by the splendidly named

Yet, when it came to dealing with servants, many Victorian people behaved in ways that appear today to be mean, hard-hearted and astonishingly unfair. Why was this?

Not like us

Although some Victorian employers behaved towards their servants with thoughtfulness and kindness, very, very few treated them as equals. Victorian books of household hints, and upper-class women's letters and diaries, make it clear that employers saw servants almost as a different species from themselves. Few went as far as writer Virginia Woolf – a child in Victorian times – who described them as being a nuisance, like 'kitchen flies', but a great many thought that the poor, lower-class men and women who worked for them were 'coarse', 'ignorant', 'clumsy' and 'unrefined'. Servants were human, yes, but they were 'not like us'.

Ladies' National Association for the Diffusion of Sanitary Knowledge, which also called for more fresh air and exercise for all housebound Victorian women, including servants.

What made Victorians think this way? Servants looked different. They had big, rough, red hands from scrubbing and cleaning, and (in the countryside) sunburnt skin from working in the fields. They wore clothes that were 'wrong' – either dull, dirty, shabby and old-fashioned, or else showy, tasteless, cheap finery. They spoke bluntly, and sometimes shockingly; they were not well educated; they did not have the manners of polite society. They could not be trusted. They were 'other'. God had placed them in a different rank in society: the lowest one.

Coarse and common

'There was another candidate for all-work service – a big-boned young Irishwoman, pleasant of speech and not ill-looking, but coarse-featured and with something about her that unmistakably bespoke a "back-slum" origin.'

London journalist James Greenwood, 1883

'If you neglect to observe the rules I shall teach you, you will always be awkward and fit only for common places and low wages.'

'Mrs Motherly', The Servants' Behaviour Book, 1859

145

Disgraceful!

'I was once in the nursery bedroom, when Anna came in, panting, with a can[1] of water. As I spoke to her, she sank down on a chair, saying, "Excuse me Ma'am, I am so tired." But I could not excuse…. [She] acted very rudely. It would have been but a small effort, to stand for a few moments, however tired…[she] might be, and girls who are not capable of such an effort are not fit for service.'

'Mrs Motherly', 1859

However, Mrs Motherly does admit that if a servant girl were to feel faint, it would be all right for her to collapse – so long as she asked permission first!

'I don't care how hard I work…but I want a place where I'm treated as though I was the same flesh and blood as my fellow creatures. I left my last place because I wasn't.'

*Maid-of-all-work interviewed by journalist
James Greenwood, 1883*

1. can: large bucket. When full, it would have been very heavy.

If willing, servants could be taught to improve – but they would always be inferiors. At the same time, their lowly nature meant that they could be treated harshly by employers, because they had been born to work harder, suffer more, own and earn less, obey their 'betters' – and not protest or complain.

In the 20th century, white people who supported the apartheid system in South Africa despised, misunderstood, feared – and exploited – black people in a surprisingly similar fashion.

Not seen, not heard

Although Victorian households relied on servants to run smoothly, many employers seem to have been strangely reluctant to acknowledge their servants' existence.

> 'Do they think that the fairies come and do the rooms, then?'
>
> *Reportedly said by a Victorian parlourmaid*

One nobleman was rumoured to dismiss any housemaid that he caught sight of after midday, because he thought that all housework should have been completed by then. In grand country houses, servants' dormitories were built with windowless walls facing gardens and terraces – or even sunk underground – so that employers strolling in the sunshine would not be overlooked by servants. Why this unwillingness?

• Partly because Victorian conventions – the unwritten rules for polite society – stipulated that people from different classes should not mix socially, although in fact many young upper-class men flirted (scandalously) with working-class women in bars, theatres and music-halls.

• Partly because keeping separate from servants avoided embarrassment and protected privacy. Servants knew too much about their employers' private lives – after all, they emptied their chamberpots and washed their underwear, by hand.

• Partly because wealthy Victorians simply did not wish to share their comfortable parlours or grand dining rooms, their cosy tea-parties or splendid dances, their music, their laughter and conversation, their meals or any of their leisure time with members of the 'lower orders'. They had almost nothing – apart from giving orders – to say to them.

Keep your distance

As well as confining their servants to the less pleasant parts of the house, Victorian employers found many other ways of keeping apart – in mind as well as body – from the people who worked for them. All helped make sure that the servants knew – and stayed in – their place in the household and in the community.

Hand objects to your employer on a small tray; this avoids any risk of hand-to-hand contact.

for servants:
How to be invisible

- Never let your voice be heard by your employers, except when necessary, and then as little as possible.

- Never start a conversation with them, unless you are delivering a message or asking a necessary question.

- Never talk to another servant, or person of your own rank, or to a child, when in the presence of your employers.

- Never talk in a passage, hall or staircase, unless strictly necessary, and then do it as briefly as possible, and in a low voice.

- Never call out from one room to another.

- Don't chatter or laugh – even in the kitchen. Sound carries all through the house.

- At family prayers, sit right at the back, close to the wall.

- Don't go into the garden, unless you are a nursemaid taking the children for a walk. That space is for your employers to enjoy, along with all the other main rooms in the house. Your place is in the kitchen, scullery, basement and attic only, except when you are working elsewhere.

- If you meet your employers in the street, don't smile. If they happen to catch your eye, nod or curtsey; otherwise, ignore them.

- At Church (where, in principle, all are equal in the eyes of God), stand back, to let your employers walk in front of you.

- If you are asked to walk outside with your mistress – for example, to carry 'a baby or a parcel' – keep several steps behind her.

- Above all – should you by some strange chance be feeling happy – don't sing!

A delicate question

You have an urgent message to deliver. But your master or mistress is on the other side of a firmly closed door. Should you fling it open and walk in boldly? Or should you knock gently, then wait for further instructions?

- Many employers find servants knocking at every door before entering extremely tiresome – and say so.

- On the other hand, if you enter a room without knocking, you might find your master or mistress getting undressed, or having a bath, or doing something even more embarrassing.

What should you, a poor servant, do? Turn the page upside down to see the answer.

If the room is private space, such as a bedroom, ALWAYS knock before entering.

If a room is public – that is, if it is used by several people, such as a parlour – there is no need to knock.

for employers:
How to stay separate from your servants

• Treat servants like children
Tell them when to get up and when to go to bed. Be nosy and bossy. Keep strict control of what they do, who they see, what they wear, and how they spend their time.

'Servants are, after all, very like children: overindulgence spoils them; and if we would make them good and useful members of our household, we must train them with all kindness, but in wholesome fear. We want them to think of *us*, to study *our* comfort.'

W. S. Gilbert, London Characters, 1870

Write rules for them to follow, as if they were at school. Some employers pin these up in the kitchen as a constant reminder. You'll be able to think of your own rules, we are sure, but over the page are some examples to get you started:

Rules for servants

1. Never speak to a lady or a gentleman without saying 'Sir' or 'Ma'am', as the case may be – or 'Master' and 'Miss' for children.

2. Always answer – 'Yes, Ma'am'; 'Very sorry, Ma'am' – when you receive an order or reproof. Don't just stand there silently, looking stupid or sullen.

3. Keep still when you are speaking or being spoken to – and keep your hands folded neatly in front of you or at your sides.

4. Always stand up when a lady or gentleman comes into the room.

5. Do not invite your friends or followers into the house without your employer's permission.

6. Don't leave the house without permission.

7. No swearing!

8. If you have free time, don't relax with a novel or a magazine. Do some sewing or mending. They're more useful.

9. Don't try to study or improve your mind. Learning's not for you (unless you are a governess).

10. Always be neat and tidy and clean. We'll be checking!

• **Undermine them**

Ignore their likes and dislikes, their personal views and wishes. Expect them to put your family's needs before their own. One servant was banned from visiting her family in case she brought germs back with her. If you choose, you can ignore the names that servants were given by their parents, and give them one of your own. You may find it easier always to have a housemaid or a footman with the same name.

• **Think of servants as if they were household objects, not people.**

It's well known that footmen who are tall and good-looking – and with shapely legs – get better wages than shorter, less attractive men. Rich employers, who can afford more than one manservant, like to hire footmen in 'matching pairs' – they look so good when opening the door to visitors, or riding behind their employer's carriage.

The same applies to ladies' maids and parlourmaids: both are on show in your home, and you like your house to look nice – so, the prettier, the better!

What's in a name?

'The first day I went there, Miss Ellen began a "Susaning" me all over the place.

'"This is how we like so-and-so done, Susan. This is how we wish t'other, Susan."

'So I says, "'Scuse me Miss, but the name of Susan don't apply to me. My name is Hadelaide – Hadelaide 'Obson,[1] Miss..."

'She says, "That's unfortunate, Hadelaide is my sister's name. Can't you do with Susan? Or there's half a dozen others you can choose from – Jane, Polly, Ann, Betsey..."'

Maid-of-all-work, interviewed in 1883

'Victoria'? Good gracious, Susan, what *were* your parents thinking of?

1. Hadelaide 'Obson = Adelaide Hobson, spoken with a Cockney (working-class London) accent. 'Adelaide' was a newly fashionable name in Victorian times, and popular with the middle and upper classes. It was too grand for a servant!

• **Keep a close eye on servants' morals.**
Some employers insist that maids and menservants attend Church with them every Sunday, regardless of the servants' own beliefs or religious traditions. And one noblewoman is even said to check that her female servants are not pregnant, by ordering the head housemaid to make a report on her colleagues every month!

An unfortunate affair

'My Mother's maid, poor Peggy Davidson,... was unable to resume her place...the reason for this Simon Ross the Butler would give, for he "had ruined her for ever".[1]...

'My Mother, a quiet woman in general,... would admit of no compromise. Ross was a good servant, a good son, a clever man, a nice looking man,...but he was an immoral man and he had outraged decency in her house and he should not remain in it unless he made Peggy..."an honest woman".'[2]

Elizabeth Grant, Memoirs of a Highland Lady
(written 1840s, published 1898)

1. *made her pregnant.*
2. *married her straight away.*

157

• **Make it clear that servants belong to you.** After all, they are members of your household! The best way of doing this is to make them wear a uniform (even though they have, of course, to buy or make their own clothes). If you're rich and grand, dress your footmen in gold-braided livery (official dress), with white stockings, buckled shoes, knee-breeches, and short, tight jackets with silver buttons bearing your family crest. Yes, of course it's old-fashioned – clothes like this were popular almost 100 years ago. But smartly turned-out servants are a very good advertisement for your family's wealth and rank – and will impress your visitors.

'I like to be waited on by a neat-handed Phillis[1] of a girl in her nice-fitting gown, and a pink ribbon in her cap.'

Spoken by a (female) character in a Victorian novel: William Thackeray, Hobson's Choice, *1842*

---

1. a poetic name for a country girl.

How to dress the part

Acceptable attire for a maid in a well-to-do household, c. 1850

White cap (a coloured ribbon is permitted)

Hair tied neatly back (no fringe)

Morning:[1] cotton print dress, often lilac

Stiff, starched collar

Afternoon: black 'stuff' (fine wool) dress

Tight waist created by whalebone corset

White apron

Black shoes (rather than boots)

For outdoor wear add a shawl and a straw bonnet

1. This is when you do your dirtiest work.

Your capsule wardrobe

Each year, you will need to buy:

- 4 pairs shoes
- 2 pairs black wool stockings
- 2 pairs white cotton stockings
- 2 gowns
- 6 aprons
- 6 caps
- bonnet, shawl, ribbons
- clogs or pattens.[1]

(You can wear last year's gowns – or even older ones – for doing dirty tasks. If you get holes in your stockings, darn them.)

'The poorer you may be, the more difficult you will find it to keep neat. This, instead of being a drawback, is really a help, inasmuch as it gives you better practice.'

'Mrs Motherly', 1859

Clogs

1. *clogs: In Britain, these were strong leather shoes with wooden soles. pattens: wooden soles, sometimes very tall, which could be attached to ordinary shoes to keep them out of the mud.*

On the other hand...

Victorian employers were undoubtedly strict with their servants, but the rules they made were intended to protect the young men and women who came to work for them, as well as to control them. At least some employers would have agreed with the Victorian writer who urged:

'Let masters and mistresses weigh well this truth, that their servants have the same passions, affections, and feelings as themselves; let them...endeavour to influence them by the same motives they would employ for the guidance of their own flesh and blood.'

W. S. Gilbert, London Characters, *1870*

Servants have feelings too!

Sniff!

Women were Widealised in Victorian Britain

'The history of service *is* the history of British women.'

Alison Light, Mrs Woolf and the Servants, *2007*

CHAPTER TEN

WORLD OF WOMEN

By late Victorian times (from around 1870), servants' lives had changed. Except in the very largest stately homes, they now worked in a world almost entirely made up of women. In ordinary middle-class households, maids-of-all-work had always had only themselves, or another female servant, for company. But now, in many large households, butlers, footmen and pageboys were being replaced by smart, neat, female parlourmaids. Even in grand country houses, where male 'outdoor' servants were still employed, they were usually kept well away from female indoor servants. One housemaid recalled the welcome 'breath of fresh air' – in every sense of the words – brought by male gardeners who arrived twice each week bringing flowers and greenery for floral decorations.

Why this change? Partly, working-class men were finding alternative jobs in factories, foundries, railways and mines. There, the work was hard and dirty, but they were free wage-earners, not submissive servants. Partly, too, Victorian ideas about home life were altering fast. Increasingly, people with money saw their homes as private, almost sacred spaces. A house was calm and quiet (like the ideal Victorian wife!) – a safe haven from the busy, dangerous, dirty, masculine world of business and industry. It was also pure (again, like a wife), both practically and morally. The 'pollution' of poverty was safely shut outside its front door, along with the disorderly public world of crime, riot, rapid change and disquieting religious, political and social quarrels. At the same time, and for the same reasons, domestic work came to be seen as 'unmanly'. Male household servants had no place in this homely women's world.

Domestic goddesses

According to Victorian poets and novelists, this calm, quiet, feminine home was the natural environment of any good middle-class woman. She was the 'Angel on the Hearth',[1] born only for 'domestic endearments and household joys'.[2] Her mission was to soothe and inspire her husband and care for her children.

(A considerable number of Victorian women saw such a home as a prison, not a refuge – and said so. But that is another story…. In any case, however personally liberated the protesting women hoped to be, they mostly still kept servants to work for them.)

The great unwashed

It was also the 'Angel's' task to guard her home and make sure that it stayed neat and clean at all times. She could not do this herself, of course. The physical work – even if she

1. the title of a poem by Coventry Patmore (a man), 1823–1896.
2. a phrase used by novelist Charlotte Brontë (a woman), 1816–1865 – only rather questioningly.

could manage it – would lower her status, and the dirt would pollute her angelic nature. She had to rely on servants: 'the daughters of the great unwashed'.[1] Back at home in the country, their families lived in squalor. They knew about dirt. They could manage.

Few real-life women could fulfil male poets' fantasies about angels, and fewer still lived like Jane Eyre (see opposite), but, as the Victorian age progressed, more and more women did stay at home – and employed female servants. Thriving Victorian businesses meant that husbands grew richer, and could afford to support a non-working wife and family. In fact, they were proud to do so; it showed that they were successful.

By 1881, almost a quarter of all English households had a servant – and almost all these were women. By 1901, at the end of Victoria's reign, one out of every three women who worked was a servant. And, among indoor servants, over 90 per cent were female.

1. Professor Mary Chamberlain made this very neat observation in 1997. The phrase 'great unwashed' is due to the aristocratic Victorian writer Edward Bulwer-Lytton (1803–1873).

Household joys?

The dramatic, romantic novel *Jane Eyre*, written by ex-governess Charlotte Brontë, caused a sensation when it was first published in 1847. It tells the story of a poor, unhappy orphan girl, Jane, who has to work as a governess to survive. She falls in love with brooding, passionate, strong-willed Mr Rochester, whose past contains a dark secret. He begs Jane to run away with him, but she refuses, and leaves his home. After many trials and tribulations, Jane receives an inheritance. The money will raise her to the status of gentlewoman (though readers already know that she has a noble heart and spirit). When Jane is asked how she will spend her time from then on, she replies (perhaps rather surprisingly to modern eyes):

'My first aim will be to clean down...Moor House from chamber to cellar; my next to rub it up with bees-wax, oil and an indefinite number of cloths, till it glitters again; my third, to arrange every chair, table, bed, carpet with mathematical precision.'

Victorian readers would interpret this passage as proof of Jane's womanly virtues. For a woman, a clean, neat house was the outward sign of inner goodness.

But Jane (now a lady) expected her servant to do a lot of the work, of course.

In short, women with money relied on female servants to work for them, so they could fulfil the Victorian dream of an 'Angel on the Hearth'. Poor women servants looked to female employers for a job, food and housing. Each depended on the other.

What men want

One Victorian advice-writer knew exactly what every husband wanted when he came home from work:

'A comfortable fire-side, well-cooked food, no disorder, no litter of any kind; keep the home free from disagreeable reminders... no talking of Susan's [the maid's] shortcomings, or of baby's ailments...'

Mrs Eliza Warren, A Young Wife's Perplexities, 1886

Cheap but not cheerful

There were two other reasons why women servants had largely replaced male ones. Firstly, females were cheaper. Although servants' pay, as compared with prices, had increased by the end of Victoria's reign, women's wages were almost always lower than men's. Employers also had to pay tax on male servants – until as recently as 1937!

Secondly, women servants – who were taught at school, at church and in books of instructions to be 'womanly', meek and mild – were probably less likely than male servants to quarrel with or cheek their employers.

'Miss P... kept me out[1] longer than I thought she ought to of [= have] done, therefore I gave her a little row for it.'

William Tayler, footman, 1837, speaking about one of his (very good) employers

Women servants were also, on the whole, less able than men to stand up for themselves if they were harshly treated. Hannah Cullwick put up with 'most disheartening' abuse from her employers.

1. accompanying her on a carriage-drive.

And, last but not least, although Victorian males were taught from boyhood to be gracious and courteous towards 'the fairer sex', women servants could conveniently seem much more 'invisible' to members of polite society than a stout, imposing male butler or a tall, handsome footman.

'The same gentleman who would stoop to pick up a lady's handkerchief would pass a maid struggling to carry an over-loaded coal scuttle without a thought that he should assist her.'

Historian Marian Ramelson

More like the sweatier sex, if you ask me.

Servant starvation...

In 1897, almost at the end of Queen Victoria's reign, London was shocked by the case of Emily Jane Popejoy. Having left home aged 16 to work for a rich, fashionable employer, Mrs Camilla Nicholls, poor Emily Jane was half-starved and frequently beaten, suffering, on separate occasions, a black eye and a broken nose. When she could stand this treatment no longer, Emily Jane escaped back to her parents' home. But by then she was so weak – she weighed only 65 lb (29.5 kg) – that she died just a few days later from pneumonia. Mrs Nicholls was sent to prison.

...and mistress murder

Even more shocking – though much less usual – was the sensational murder in 1879 of Surrey widow Mrs Thomas by her Irish maid Kate Webster. After being dismissed for slovenly work – a sin as well as an error, in Victorian eyes – Kate got drunk, waited for Mrs Thomas to return from church, ambushed her, beat her to death, chopped the body into pieces, and boiled them. Kate was hanged.

Times have changed

'A very independent spirit
is a marked characteristic of the
lower classes of servants...'

*Social reporters Charles Booth
and Jessie Argyle, 1903*

CHAPTER ELEVEN

END OF AN ERA

In 1864, during the first half of Queen Victoria's reign, maid-of-all-work Hannah Cullwick reported a very insulting incident. She was crawling on her hands and knees, sweeping a carpet, when a young lady approached her. The lady wanted Hannah to put a clean rug on the floor of her bedroom. But, instead of speaking quietly or even shouting her orders, she simply pointed at the rug, and kicked Hannah with her foot.

That kind of behaviour was not considered 'ladylike' even in the 1860s, but by the time that Victoria died, nearly forty years later in 1901, it would have been completely unacceptable – especially to servants. So would countless other demands made by earlier Victorian employers. These included sending servant boys to run errands with murderous packages of poison (see opposite), heartlessly banning servants from visiting dying parents to say a last goodbye, or requiring them – like Charles Darwin's faithful butler – to shower their master's lower body with cold water every day (a four-month 'cure' for diarrhoea), then dry him, and clean up afterwards.

A few particularly mean-spirited employers even set traps to test – or tempt – the honesty of their poorly paid servants, by leaving marked coins around the house, then checking to see whether the servants had pocketed them.

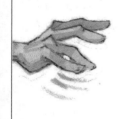

The peculiar case of the Chocolate Cream Poisoner

In Brighton in the late 1860s, a rich, pretty, lonely, passionate – and insane – spinster, Christiana Edmunds, fell in love with her medical advisor, Dr Beard. She wrote him love-letters, and he foolishly replied. But Dr Beard was married! News of the letters could ruin his career. He asked Christiana to stop writing.

In 1870, Christiana began to send errand boys on mysterious missions. Their task was to fetch poison (to kill stray cats, Christiana said) from nearby chemists', and chocolates from a well-known local sweet-shop. Secretly adding the poison to the chocolates, Christiana took a box to Dr Beard's wife, who became very sick, but recovered.

Next year, Christiana sent a poisoned fruitcake to Mrs Beard (her servants ate it, and were lucky to survive). She also smuggled poisoned chocolates into the sweet-shop, where anyone could buy them.[1] Soon, a child ate one and died. Dr Beard, now suspicious, contacted the police.

Christiana was arrested, but nothing could be proved until a servant boy told how she had sent him to fetch poison. Convicted of murder in 1872, Christiana spent the rest of her life in gaol.

1. She claimed that the chocolates had been sent to her in error, and she was therefore returning them – by errand boy.

Rights and rewards

However, by 1901, such outrageous demands by employers belonged (mostly) to the past. Now, at the beginning of the new, more democratic, 20th century, men and women servants were no longer prepared to be treated like a separate – and very inferior – species. They were demanding their rights!

'By our Industry[1] we Live. Unity is Strength.'

Slogan of the London and Provincial Domestic Servants' Union, founded 1891

New servants' demands (set out by firebrand Glasgow campaigner Jessie Stephen in 1911) included a guaranteed minimum wage, regular holidays, at least one day off each fortnight, and the right to refuse dangerous tasks, such as cleaning the outside of big upstairs windows – without a ladder!

Just as importantly, Victorian ideas about service began to change…

1. *hard work.*

How would you serve?

For most of the Victorian age, men and women, rich and poor, believed that 'serving others' was a good, moral, religious thing to do. (That is why Victorians called the people who ran the government 'civil servants', rather than 'state staff', or similar.) But ways of 'serving' varied, according to class, wealth and gender:

• Are you a grand, rich, noble lady?
Then hold a lavish dinner-party to charm important foreign businessmen. You'll serve your country by encouraging visitors to make trade deals that will benefit British industries.

• Or are you a poor farm-servant lad, getting up at 5.00 a.m. every day to feed the plough-horses and muck out their stables?

Remember, without you, land could not be ploughed, wheat could not be grown, bread could not be made, and people would go hungry. That's service, too!

By 1901, fewer boys from poor families wanted to trudge through the mud as farmhands, or dress up in antiquated knee-breeches and fetch and carry as footmen. Fewer country girls flocked to London to work day and night as cooks, cleaners and nurserymaids. And, instead of complaining about their servants' poor performance, rich women in 1901 worried whether they could find any servants at all. In fact, there was a 'servant shortage'!

As a result, servants' wages were rising, compared with the overall cost of living. This meant that some people could no longer afford to employ a live-in domestic help. In 1901, a smaller proportion of families had servants than in 1851: around one in six, rather than one in four. Even so, there were still more people working as servants than in any other kind of job – except farm labourers. But times were changing fast.

More choice, greater freedom

Working-class youngsters now had a wider choice of occupations than ever before.

For boys, work in factories, foundries, mines, railways, offices, and in new technology (such as electric light and the telephone) seemed more interesting and exciting than being a servant. It was also better paid – and workers had fixed hours (which meant free time to call their own), and did not have to live in their employers' homes.

For girls, shops, offices, factories, schools, hospitals, and respectable restaurants and coffee houses also offered higher wages and greater freedom. Even if a girl happened to like housework, she could now perform domestic duties in new and different ways:

- **Charwomen (cleaners) visited houses to scrub, clean and polish for a few hours daily or weekly.**

- Steam laundries collected dirty clothes from each household and delivered them again, neatly washed and ironed.

- New cookery books and domestic training colleges tried to teach women how to cook for themselves – with mixed results, admittedly.

- Thanks to Florence Nightingale and others, professional nurses now cared for the sick and for young babies, at home or in hospital.

- Dressmakers and hat-shops (many run by women) created and repaired fashionable garments; the world's first paper patterns and domestic sewing machines (both invented in the USA) made it quicker and easier for middle-class women to sew their own clothes.

- New illustrated newspapers – and exciting displays in new department-store windows – offered style advice. And shops were full of new, mass-produced soaps, shampoos and cosmetics. So who needed a lady's maid?

- Most important of all, new household machines – if employers could afford them – made it possible to complete housework in record time, and with less physical effort – and many fewer servants.

The end of housework?

Some great Victorian domestic inventions:

1860 Linoleum, the first synthetic floor covering – hygienic and easy to clean.

1868 Gas water heater: instant hot water on tap!

1876 Carpet sweeper: no more need for brushes and beaters.

1876 Telephone: no need for errand boys or footmen. Now you can communicate with your friends, and give orders to tradesmen, from the comfort of your home.

1879 Electric light bulb: dazzling!

1880 Refrigerated meat, shipped from Australia: cheap, fresh and plentiful.

1882 Electric safety iron; easy to heat, with precise controls.

1885 Gas mantle. Gives out heat and glows white-hot. Let there be light!

Electric iron

1889 Electric oven: cooking at the flick of a switch!

1901 Vacuum cleaner. Whoosh that dust away!

And coming soon:

1907 Electric washing machine. Goodbye washday blues!

1910 Electric mixing machine: like a mechanical kitchen maid.

The professionals

New skills, common amongst even the poorest by 1901, also increased job opportunities. Reading, writing and mathematics were taught to all British children from the 1870s. Although many left school to start work at 14 (because their families could no longer support them), others went on to study. Boys became apprentices, girls learned housekeeping at new domestic colleges. Slowly, the average age of servants increased; they no longer began work as poor, scared, powerless children, but as trained young adults. Increasingly they saw themselves as professionals, with valuable skills to sell. They would work hard at all kinds of exhausting, dirty, boring jobs – but they would *not* be patronised. After all, their employers depended on them – and they knew it!

For this reason, some historians have called Victorian servants 'the first modern workforce'. Although many servants lived solitary, shadowy, downtrodden lives, they were not slaves. Their rights as free citizens were protected by law; they could not lawfully be imprisoned or beaten. They earned money wages, to spend as they chose, as well as board and lodging. Their work was governed by legally binding contracts. They were free to give notice, and leave any job. They had specialist skills, and were proud of them.

By the end of Victoria's reign, many nervous or sensitive employers were finding these confident, self-respecting servants difficult to deal with. Servants saw masters and mistresses at close quarters every day, and knew their most intimate family secrets. But cooks and maids and nannies and chauffeurs and footmen and gardeners no longer pretended to be invisible, or to have no thoughts or feelings of their own. Servants were now a powerful presence in any household that employed them. They might be calm and efficient, or slovenly and bad-tempered – beloved family 'treasures' or costly, exasperating 'burdens' – but no-one could ignore them.

Glossary*

It's Very Peculiar how many of these words are to do with social class – a Victorian obsession!

adhere Agree with, follow.

appointed Organised, planned, set up.

arbitrary Without any logical reason.

blacklead Sticky black polish used to clean cast-iron grates and ranges.

bonbons (French) Bite-sized sweets, sometimes dusted in powdered sugar or wrapped in decorative paper.

caste (Indian) Position in society.

chignon Elaborate upswept hairstyle for women.

compote Dessert of fruit gently cooked in syrup.

conventions Unwritten rules for polite or acceptable behaviour.

culinary Concerned with cooking.

demeanour Appearance and behaviour.

docile Gentle and easily led.

domestic Concerned with houses and housekeeping.

estate Position in society.

etiquette Good manners; the correct way to behave in polite society.

footman Male servant (usually young) who opened doors, took messages, waited at table and accompanied a master or mistress when they left the house on business or to go visiting.

galantine Dish of cold meat, often set in savoury jelly.

gallant Very polite, admiring and helpful to women.

gentry Rich, land-owning men and women, usually connected to ancient noble families.

grate Part of a fireplace: a metal basket to hold burning wood or coal.

husbandry An old-fashioned word for farming.

integrity Honesty and trustworthiness.

livery Old-fashioned uniform worn by male servants.

* Words that are defined in the text are not repeated here.

omnibus Horsedrawn coach that ran along a fixed route in a town or city. Any member of the public could buy a ticket to ride on it.

perquisites Extra rewards for their work taken by senior servants. Traditionally, top butlers took one bottle in every six as a 'perk', for example.

prevailing mode The latest fashions.

propriety 'Proper' (suitable, acceptable) behaviour.

range A large cast-iron kitchen stove, with hotplates, ovens and (sometimes) a boiler for heating water. It usually burned coal, and had to be cleaned out and relit every day.

roasting jack An adjustable metal hook for hanging meat to roast over an open fire.

satirical Criticising by making jokes.

scullion Servant (usually female) who did rough, dirty cleaning and dishwashing in the kitchens.

servants' hall Dining room and common room where servants in large households could relax when off duty. It was often shut off from rooms used by employers and their guests behind a door padded with thick green baize (woollen cloth). This muffled noise, and was a symbol of the division between servants and employers.

soirée Evening party.

spheres Different ranks in society.

station of life Position in society.

transferable Able to be passed from one owner to another.

turnspit Kitchen machine that turned a spit (a pole on which meat was fixed to roast) over a large open fire.

tweeny 'In-between' maid: a junior servant who helped with house-cleaning and in the kitchen.

under servant Junior servant.

upper servant Senior servant.

upright Well-behaved, honest.

valet (French) Personal manservant with special responsibility for his master's clothes.

vexations Annoyances.

Timeline of servant history

1777 UK government taxes employers of male servants. The money will help fight North American colonists, who have just (1776) declared Independence.

1782–1792 Employers of women servants are also taxed.

1819 onwards Factory Acts improve conditions in factories and mines, but do not protect servants.

1825 Former servants Sarah and Samuel Adams publish *The Complete Servant*, a very idealised guide to servants' tasks. Many other books of advice follow.

1834 New Poor Law. All poor people – including children – who cannot pay for food and shelter are taken to local workhouses, where they are treated almost like prisoners.

1837 Victoria becomes queen of the United Kingdom. *The Servants' Magazine* is first published, advising servants to work hard and be good.

1842 Child labour is finally outlawed in factories, but children still work as servants.

1846 Servants' Benevolent Institution founded to help old, ill and unemployed serving men and women.

1847 The Mayhew brothers publish a humorous book about troublesome servants: *The Greatest Plague of Life*.

1850s Trades unions campaign to win better pay and conditions for workers in many industries, but do not (yet) protect servants.

1851 First detailed census reveals that there are over a million indoor servants in Britain. Apprentices and Servants Act: employers of servants under 18 must give them adequate food, lodging and clothing.

1859 'Mrs Motherly' publishes *The Servant's Behaviour Book*, urging servants to be modest and obedient.

1861 Mrs Beeton's *Book of Household Management* describes how to manage servants.

1869 Tax on hair powder abolished. (The only people who still wore hair powder were liveried footmen.)

1870 New Education Act makes primary schooling compulsory for all UK children.

1872 First servants' trade unions set up, in Dundee, Scotland, and Leamington, in the English Midlands.

1876 Queen Victoria becomes Empress of India.

1889 British social researcher Seebohm Rowntree writes that employing a servant puts families into the 'middle class'.

1891 Britain has almost 2 million indoor servants.

1897 Victoria's Diamond Jubilee (celebration of 60 years as queen). Britain is the world's greatest power.

1890s Employers in northern England recruit servants from Germany and Scandinavia, because young north-English people prefer to work in factories.

1891 London and Provincial Domestic Servants' Union campaigns for better pay and conditions.

1899 Board of Trade report on servants' wages shows older, skilled servants much better paid than juniors.

1900 The Duke of Portland employs 320 servants at Welbeck Abbey. This may be a record! Fewer middle-class families keep servants than in 1880.

1901 Queen Victoria dies. The new Queen, Alexandra, organises tea-parties for thousands of female servants to celebrate her husband's coronation as Edward VII.

1906 New edition of Mrs Beeton's book shows that wages expected by trained, experienced servants are almost 30 per cent higher than in 1861.

1908 Old-age pensions are paid to workers over 70, saving many elderly servants from extreme poverty.

1910 Domestic Workers' Union of Great Britain formed.

1911 National Insurance Act provides some medical care and unemployment pay for servants who pay weekly insurance contributions.

1914–1918 World War I. Almost all young men servants join the armed forces. By 1918, 1 in 4 female servants has also left domestic service. Many do the work of men, such as driving buses or fire-fighting.

1919–1923 Many women refuse to work as servants after the war has ended. The government sets up committees to report on the 'domestic service problem'.

1937 Tax on employers of male servants abolished.

Index

A servant's
nightmare

Very Peculiar Histories™

Ancient Egypt
Mummy Myth and Magic
Jim Pipe
ISBN: 978-1-906714-92-5

The Blitz
David Arscott
ISBN: 978-1-907184-18-5

Brighton
David Arscott
ISBN: 978-1-906714-89-5

Castles
Jacqueline Morley
ISBN: 978-1-907184-48-2

Christmas
Fiona Macdonald
ISBN: 978-1-907184-50-5

Global Warming
Ian Graham
ISBN: 978-1-907184-51-2

Great Britons
Ian Graham
ISBN: 978-1-907184-59-8

Ireland
Jim Pipe
ISBN: 978-1-905638-98-7

London
Jim Pipe
ISBN: 978-1-907184-26-0

Rations
David Arscott
ISBN: 978-1-907184-25-3

Scotland
Fiona Macdonald

Vol. 1: From ancient times
to Robert the Bruce
ISBN: 978-1-906370-91-6

Vol. 2: From the Stewarts
to modern Scotland
ISBN: 978-1-906714-79-6

The Tudors
Jim Pipe
ISBN: 978-1-907184-58-1

Vampires
Fiona Macdonald
ISBN: 978-1-907184-39-0

Wales
Rupert Matthews
ISBN: 978-1-907184-19-2

Yorkshire
John Malam
ISBN: 978-1-907184-57-4

Heroes, Gods and Monsters of
Ancient Greek Mythology
Michael Ford
ISBN: 978-1-906370-92-3

Heroes, Gods and Monsters of
Celtic Mythology
Fiona Macdonald
ISBN: 978-1-905638-97-0

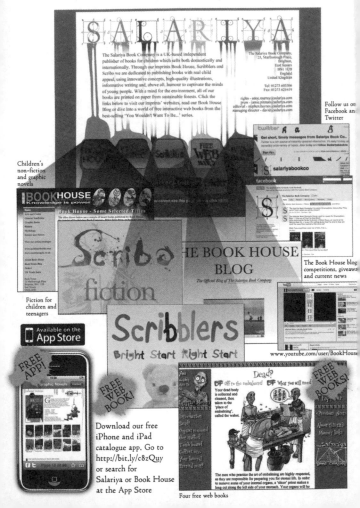

www.salariya.com
where books come to life!

The Salariya Book Company is a UK-based independent publisher of books for children which sells both domestically and internationally. Through our imprints Book House, Scribblers and Scribo we are dedicated to publishing books with real child appeal, using innovative concepts, high-quality illustrations, informative writing and, above all, humour to captivate the minds of young people. With a mind for the environment, all of our books are printed on paper from sustainable forests. Click the links below to visit our imprints' websites, read our Book House Blog or dive into a world of free interactive web books from the best-selling 'You Wouldn't Want To Be...' series.

The Salariya Book Company,
25, Marlborough Place,
Brighton,
East Sussex
BN1 1UB
England
United Kingdom

Tel: 01273 603306
Fax: 01273 621619

rights - anne.murray@salariya.com
press - jamie.pitman@salariya.com
editorial - stephen.haynes@salariya.com
managing director - david@salariya.com

Follow us on Facebook and Twitter

Children's non-fiction and graphic novels

Fiction for children and teenagers

The Book House blog competitions, giveaways and current news

www.youtube.com/user/BookHouse

Available on the App Store

FREE APP!

FREE WEB BOOK!

Download our free iPhone and iPad catalogue app. Go to http://bit.ly/c8zQuy or search for Salariya or Book House at the App Store

FREE WEB BOOKS!

Four free web books